Charlotte Crosby is one of the nation's best-loved and funniest TV stars. Her previous memoirs, *Me, Me, Me* and *Brand New Me*, were both number one *Sunday Times* hardback bestsellers. She is also the winner of 2013's *Celebrity Big Brother*, the creator of two hugely successful fitness DVDs, the star of BBC's *Charlotte in Sunderland* and an ambassador for the Ectopic Pregnancy Trust.

Also by Charlotte Crosby:

Me Me Me
Live Fast, Lose Weight
Brand New Me
Charlotte Crosby's 30 Day Blitz

Me, myself & mini me

CHARLOTTE CROSBY

HEADLINE

First published in 2023 by
HEADLINE PUBLISHING GROUP

First published in paperback in 2024 by
HEADLINE PUBLISHING GROUP

1

Cataloguing in Publication Data is available from the British Library

ISBN 978 1 0354 0145 1

All photographs courtesy of the author.

Typeset in Berling and Shakies by CC Book Production
Printed and bound in Great Britain by Clays Ltd, Elcograf S.p.A.

The information contained in this book is not intended to replace the
services of trained medical professionals or to be a substitute for medical advice.
You are advised to consult a doctor on any matters relating to your child's or
your own health, and in particular on any matters that may require
diagnosis or medical attention.

MIX
Paper | Supporting
responsible forestry
FSC® C104740

Headline's policy is to use papers that are natural, renewable and recyclable products
and made from wood grown in well-managed forests and other controlled sources.
The logging and manufacturing processes are expected to conform to
the environmental regulations of the country of origin.

HEADLINE PUBLISHING GROUP
An Hachette UK Company
Carmelite House
50 Victoria Embankment
London EC4Y 0DZ

www.headline.co.uk
www.hachette.co.uk

In loving memory of Nana Jean

Contents

When you're pregnant, everything you read seems to be obsessed with the size of the baby. All the books and blogs are like: 'Week 4, your baby is now the size of a poppy seed . . . Week 10, your baby is the size of a kumquat . . .' (I mean, *what even the actual hell is a kumquat*?! Sounds like sperm to me – maybe that's where it came from!) So, with that in mind I've decided to go with baby themes for the chapters of this book. Although they obviously have a slight Charlotte Crosby spin on them. Here we go!

Introduction: I'm back!   1

Prologue: What I imagine giving birth will be like   3

1   *My baby is* . . . already in my mind because I am a master manifester   7

2   *My baby is* . . . not yet a reality because I am too busy with bad ex-boyfriends and being a boss business bitch   23

Contents

3 *My baby is* . . . hiding behind closed doors   37
   while I cough and splutter A LOT

4 *My baby is* . . . just around the corner   57
   because I am about to meet Jake Ankers –
   the love of my life and my ONE AND ONLY

5 *My baby is* . . . the best news ever   79

6 *My baby is* . . . hard to keep a secret   97

7 *My baby is* . . . a ray of light   109
   among some dark clouds

8 *My baby is* . . . a big surprise   121
   for the *Geordie Shore* OGs

9 *My baby is* . . . going to learn to deal with trolls   135

10 *My baby is* . . . the best excuse for a holiday   155
   and ANOTHER party

11 *My baby is* . . . giving me rollercoaster hormones   167

12 *My baby is* . . . keeping me awake at night   183

13 *My baby is* . . . the size of a melon   197
   and she's on her way OUT

14 *My baby is* . . . here and she's coming home   209

15 *My baby is* . . . the living angel of my Nana Jean   223

Contents

16 *My baby is* . . . growing and changing   237
    all the time (and so am I)

17 *My baby is* . . . a miracle, and I   255
    can't wait for more

And finally: What people think of me . . .   267
and my response!

Acknowledgements   273

Introduction:
I'm back!

Welcome back to another book,
This one is different – just take a look,
It's not stuck in the past or full of gobbledeegook.
Not even about fitness or what to cook,
This one is by far better than any other!!!
Because this is the one I became a mother . . .

Hello, friends! I'm back! Can you believe I've been in people's lives and on TV for twelve years? Wow. It blows my mind to think people still care what I've got to say and what I'm up to. So firstly – THANK YOU for sticking by me, and secondly – thank you for buying this, my THIRD autobiography. I promise you won't regret your purchase! It'll be much more fun than buying a bag – unless of course, you're getting one from my very own brand, Pepper Girls Club. In which case you can carry this book *inside* your bag, along with a nice Mars Bar cake (if you know, you *know*) and the world will be your oyster. (Whatever the hell that means. *Why would you want the world to be an oyster?!*) Anyway, here we are once again and, as ever, I promise to let you into my maddest moments, most personal life events and most intimate thoughts.

It's so crazy to think how far I've come. And to think I once wanted to be an archaeologist! *Jurassic Park* used to feel like the ideal dream job for me, I was so obsessed with dinosaurs it was untrue. And then I landed up on *Geordie Shore*. You might say, I went from dino bones to real-life neanderthals in the *Geordie Shore* house!

Prologue:
what I imagine giving birth will be like . . .

At the time of writing this part of the book, it's exactly two days and twelve hours until I'm going to HAVE AN ACTUAL BABY. I'm slumped on the sofa sucking on my eight-hundredth orange Mr Freeze ice pop – in the apartment in south-west London I've been staying in for the last four weeks with my amazing boyfriend and baby-daddy Jake. (I wanted Mr Okaro, who had looked after me when I had the ectopic pregnancy in 2016, to be my doctor for the birth. This meant having the baby privately in London, so we'd moved down a few weeks before my due date in case I went into labour early.) When we found out that Mr Okaro also works at the Portland Hospital we were over the moon and decided to have the baby there, I was determined to make sure I was going to be in the absolute best place possible. I'm so lucky to be able to afford to give birth in such an amazing hospital; I keep forgetting I'm not going to stay in a four-star hotel! I've been living on barely two hours sleep a night for the past month (literally *everything* aches all the time and I have to wee about twelve hundred times a night) so I'm desperately hoping that when I have the baby, I'm going to get some pampering and relaxation time.

P.S. Me mam has just been on the phone and when I told her that I think the Portland is going to be like a mini-break, she laughed, 'You're having a *baby*, Charlotte – what do you think is going to happen? You're not going to get handed a cocktail and caviar!'

She shouldn't be laughing though – as, if you recall, THIS is how I described my own birth into the world in my very first book . . .

The woman is hot, she's sweating. The camera pans to her vagina, everyone's stressed and panicking around her and all of a sudden, music blares and out emerges . . . Charlotte Crosby. I'm like super baby (think Stewie from *Family Guy*). I'm wearing really cool high heels. Nothing fazes me. People around are still flapping at what's happened. But without even looking round behind me, I hand me mam a tissue to wipe her brow. Then a hand comes into shot to spray my hair, someone puts some lipstick on me . . . I walk closer to the camera and then I wink, flick my hair and say, 'Because I'm worth it.'

So, now aged thirty-two years of age, this is how I imagine giving birth to my first child is going to play out:

All beautifully made up, hair washed and blow dried, I will check in about 8am and pre-order room service on the menu so it's waiting for me when I've given birth. I'll be having lobster mac and cheese from the à la carte menu, washed down with a glass of Captain Morgan's Spiced Rum (don't judge me, but I don't really like champagne) because I'm *finally* allowed to drink.

I'll have the baby while listening to a specially compiled playlist of my most favourite (some might say slightly depressing – I say *melancholy*) songs which includes Coldplay's 'Yellow' and Billie Eilish's 'Ocean Eyes' (see page 164 for my full list and run down) and she will pop out in perfect time to Norah Jones's 'Sunrise'. She's going to have a full head of flowing hair (not just round the back like an eighty-year-old man) and she's going to sleep for hours and just be perfect!

We will be wrapped up in a big bubble of love for days and, because I don't want to breastfeed, Jake will do loads of the bottle feeds throughout the night and I'll get plenty of rest (in between fine dining on my three-course meals from the hospital restaurant). It's going to be like an absolutely beautiful dream ...

AHHHHH BLISS . . .

OK, OK, let's pause for a bit. Because that's all really just very wishful thinking – because I am actually, *really* genuinely SHITTING MYSELF.

1

My baby is . . .

already in my mind because
I am a master manifester!

I admit this chapter might be short and, if I'm brutally honest with you, could be missing a bit of *actual* substance. But please just go with it and indulge me because this chapter is about my skills as a manifester and the fact that I – Charlotte Letitia Crosby – have actually been manifesting the shit out of my life ever since I was a young girl – WAY, WAY, WAY before the word 'manifest' was even a thing. When I first heard the word years ago, I thought it just meant a truck-load of fit men at a festival (which could also be a very good thing). But now it's everywhere and all over TikTok.

My twelve-year-old self would have had her mind BLOWN

by TikTok. In fact, I think I sort of manifested TikTok around that age – I used to be obsessed with filming funny videos with me mates on my phone, except it was a Sony Ericsson flip phone with a teeny tiny camera. We would literally spend hours doing silly skits where we'd pretend to be different characters and make up songs.

I honestly think I've got a skill when it comes to manifesting stuff and making things happen. I always had premonitions and they just *somehow* came true. I had a book that I'd carry with me everywhere and I'd write all my dreams in it. One was a recurring dream that I was going to be famous. I wrote it down so many times that I think the universe just got sick of me and thought, 'Oh, go on then! Have it!' I also used the book as a bit of a gratitude diary – something that is now VERY ON TREND! I'd say how grateful I was for things that had happened to me – like thanking the guy in the shop down the road for serving me alcopops when I was underage, me mates for making me laugh, and a little thanks to God for giving me pubes that didn't grow all the way down my legs so I didn't have to spend a fortune on razors. You know, all the important stuff.

Anyway, there I was, aged twelve, writing in a page of my special book, which I didn't realise was a manifesting book at the time, but it was. AND NOW, AGED THIRTY-TWO, SOMEONE NEEDS TO GIVE ME A CERTIFICATE OF INVENTION OR SOMETHING.

Reading it back, I think I was limiting myself and my ambitions a little bit, because I simply wanted to eat sushi and go skinny dipping. I should really have been dreaming much bigger. But still, I have tried both of those things, I can report they were great and all I'd ever hoped for – so that's another manifestation win!

A flashback to my twenty-five-year-old self and my 'life plan'

Before I sat down to write this book, I had a flick back through the very first book I brought out back in 2015. I was twenty-five when I wrote *Me Me Me*. I REALLY thought I had it all figured out back then! But even though most of it is way off, what's funny is that some of the stuff I put in my 'life plan' has actually come true and fallen into the right time frame!

Here's a reminder of my twenty-five-year life plan (and my analysis of its accuracy!):

1. Age twenty-six: Have my own house.

GOOD WORK! I actually did get my own house around this age, maybe a year later than I'd predicted but that's a good job, pretty spot on.

2. Age twenty-seven: Engaged (to Mitch).

NOT AT ALL CORRECT! Ha ha! Well this is REALLY funny. I have had about five boyfriends since Mitch so there's no way I was getting engaged to him! But now I've found *the one* so the journey was all worth it.

3. Age twenty-eight: I need to be married (to Mitch) because in a couple of years I'll start trying for a baby.

WRONG, WRONG, WRONG! I am not married to Mitch – thank God! Otherwise, I wouldn't be with the love of my life Jake now, who was definitely worth the wait! If I'd been married to Mitch at twenty-eight, I'd never have met Jake at a party that was celebrating sofas aged thirty-one. (Random, I know . . . and much more on this later!)

4. Age thirty: Pregnant. If it's a boy, we'll call him Ted. If it's a girl she'll be Letitia after me mam.

SEMI WRONG. I actually got pregnant much sooner, just a year after I wrote this book. As most of you know, it was the scariest time of my life as it was ectopic and I could have died. It was also a bad time because it was with my other ex, Gary. But then I finally conceived with the right man when I was thirty-one years old. So, all in all, this is not a bad guess. But I don't know where the hell I got the name Ted from!? And as for the girl's name – I mean I love me mam, and her name does run in the family, but I was never going to call my little girl Letitia!

5. I'll hopefully have my own reality TV show by then (Holly has to be in it, too) and I'll let them film all the birthing scenes like they do in *Keeping up with the Kardashians*. Saying that, I can't watch *One Born Every Minute*. It's worse than any horror film I've ever watched in my entire life.

GOLD STAR ON THIS PREDICTION! This all came true as I actually got three different reality shows of my own – *The Charlotte Crosby Experience*, MTV's *The Charlotte Show* and now my new one, *Charlotte in Sunderland*, for the BBC. And what's more, for the new one they filmed the actual birth. A whole camera set up in the place!

6. **Age thirty–thirty-two: I'll take two years off to have the parent–child bonding thing.**

NOT QUITE RIGHT. I'm thirty-two now and, much as I'd like to take two years off, I'm a working mam these days!

7. **Age forty: Loads of plastic surgery.**

OH MY GOD WHAT WAS I THINKING?! I thought forty was dead old when I wrote this and that I'd need a full-on facelift by then, like Joan Rivers (probably not the best facial role model, if I'm honest!). Admittedly I have had a nose job and a boob job (but that was mainly to correct my symmastia – or 'uniboob' as some papers called it) and I did have my lips done . . . although motherhood made me do a reverse turn on those. I know forty's still a fair few years away, but it's still definitely not quite the full works!

8. Age fifty: Possibly move to Australia.

NICE ONE! That's still on the cards actually. I'd love to be so rich I could fly all my family out to Oz as I love it there so much. So you never know. I genuinely think I could be living out in Australia by the time I'm fifty. I have two online businesses that I started around two years ago, and I want to get them to the point where I can sell them for a lot of money. I've given myself a ten-year limit for that – it's all based around the big plan. Watch this space!

All in all, I think that's not a bad effort from twenty-five-year-old me – I reckon I'd mark myself three-and-a-half out of eight.

I'm going to do another list at the end of this book so I can look back on it when I'm fifty and see if I'm the great psychic manifester I think I am!

Manifesting motherhood

Further evidence of my manifestation skills has come in the form of my baby Alba. I always knew I was going to have a girl – even before I got pregnant. I genuinely reckon it's because I manifested it for so long that it was always going to happen!

Like when we were doing an advert for MTV's *The Charlotte Show*, about four years ago now, and there were loads of props on set – all girlie things – and one of them was a giant dolls' house. It was sitting on the floor and at the end I said to one of the crew, 'Can I take that dolls' house home for my little girl please?' They looked at me a bit strangely, knowing I didn't have kids, but let me lug it all the way back home on the train. It has been sitting in my house ever since, waiting for its big moment when Alba finally falls in love with it! Isn't that just SPOOKY?!

I wonder if I can manifest my way to being a brilliant mother and having a really well-behaved and amazing-mannered daughter?! When I think about all the stuff I used to get up to when I was younger, I am looking at it all through very different eyes now and realising me mam and dad were ACTUAL SAINTS to put up with me. Not only did I fall asleep drunk on that roof at my parents' house, I would crash out in the most random places and have to phone me mates up to rescue me – like the time I fell asleep in a bush on the side of the road and Melissa had to come and collect me and found me there lying sideways next to a bike with only one wheel. I never worried about consequences or being told off, I just did what I wanted.

I am now worried about all the things Alba's going to get up to if she ends up being like me! Like when I used to go out and drink on the street aged THIRTEEN! I do not want my child hanging about on street corners! And even though I never smoked, I still had a few puffs when I was with me mates because I thought it was cool. I don't want her smoking – or VAPING for that matter (which is even worse than smoking in my opinion). Whenever I drive along and and see children with vapes in their mouth it makes me so angry – they think it's fine because it comes in different flavours like strawberries and blueberries. But it's still really bad for you!

But how the hell am I going to get her to stop doing anything if she's like I was? I have decided that bribery is the only answer. Basically, I will have to tell her, 'If you don't vape then I'll buy you a new pair of shoes.' The problem is it will no doubt end up getting more and more ridiculous as time goes on and it's not as if I can offer to buy her a superyacht so she doesn't drink in the park!

Jake will definitely be more strict because he says he wants Alba to learn how to do stuff like making the bed and to help out around the house like he had to do when he was young. He thinks that's important because she needs to know respect. But Jake's so emotional and loving and caring I think he'll end up giving her everything she wants – basically he will spoil her stupid!

I really want her to be honest with me and not lie like I did. I know it sounds bad, and people might judge me for this, but when she's sixteen, if she wants to have friends over on a Friday I'm going to let them have a few alcopops – only the 3 per cent alcopops, mind you – as I would rather she tasted alcohol when I'm around than fall asleep in a bush on the side of the road. At least I know she would be safe. Besides, alcopops are disgusting so I'm hoping this cunning plan will just put her off for life!

If I was to try to bottle up my manifesting skills and share them with you, I would say you just need to breathe it in and believe. It might sound mad, but whenever I go on holiday, I like to stand by the edge of the ocean, look at the waves lapping on the shore, and think deep thoughts about my future and what I want in life – then I imagine flinging those things into the ocean. It's as if the sea will somehow take care of it all – carry my wishes out, make it all magically happen. I also just tell the sea how grateful I am because it's important to say 'thanks' in life, as well as 'please'. The ocean just feels so powerful, like it can do anything you ask it to.

A Letter To My Younger Self

Dear Younger Charlotte

As I am now older and wiser and about to have a child (I KNOW! IT'S MAD!), I have been spending time looking back at you (well, me!) and the things you/I did and it's making me riddled with anxiety!

LOL – WHAT A STUPID WILD GIRL YOU WERE/ARE!

Our poor mother. Jesus, I can only hope my daughter will not be as absolutely feral as you/me (sh*t, this talking to myself in the past is getting really confusing!)! You really were a handful. I know I've said it a thousand times, but thank God you decided to go into *Geordie Shore* because (believe it or not, readers!) that truly did calm you down.

Eighteen-year-old Charlotte will be sat, reading this letter, drunk on a roof somewhere, having climbed out of bed in protest at Mam and Dad. Well GET DOWN NOW! Go to bed, have a big glass of water, because you are going to need a clear head when you read this next part of the letter from your older and wiser self.

Life is about to get crazy! But in a good way. It's nothing you're not used to – as we all know you love a drama (in fact the fire engine is probably on its way to you right now to get you off the roof). You are going to get your heart broken A LOT on this journey but it will all be worth it and make sense in the end. It's all part of what's meant to happen and will teach you so much important stuff – so trust in the process and just kiss the frogs (or should I say rodents!). You will experience a lot of pain, and you will have some major lows, but all I can tell you is, please keep being yourself. Don't change anything – no matter what anyone says. You are crazy but kind of lovable.

Lots of love

Charlotte xxx

P. S. STOP ARGUING WITH MAM AND DAD ALL THE TIME! You will come to realise they are your best friends in the whole world. Even though Mam did send you to school without any knickers on once, you need to get over that.

Some Notes from Me Mam Letitia About her Daughter Charlotte Letitia (AKA Me)

1. As a young child Charlotte slept so much! Even on Christmas Day she would sleep in most of the day – she wouldn't even get up when people came to visit to bring her presents.

2. Charlotte had an imaginary friend called Polly who she would say sat on her hand when she had a poo and they'd have a chat.

3. I think Charlotte was so normal and boring as a child that by the time her teenage years came along she went wild. She was a nightmare! When she was sixteen she was crazy. Vile! When she got onto *Geordie Shore* I felt like I was being given a break, like I was able to hand her over to other people for six or seven weeks at a time and they would have to look after her and try to keep her out of trouble! Saying that, as the series went on, I'd still end up having phone calls from the producers about once a show – 'Charlotte's bashed her head on something and had to go to A&E, she's run away, she's tried to jump off the jetty, you need to speak to her.'

4. Charlotte would go out and not come back for days,
    she wouldn't answer her phone – and when she did
    come home she would have such an attitude when
    we tried to ground her! We'd tell her she had to stay
    in and then the next minute she'd escape through a
    window and be out again. Once she tried to stay at
    her mate's house but her mate's mam kicked her out.
    But, instead of coming home, she lived in her car for a
    week. She was so stubborn. She was crazy, she's never
    really been a normal child.

5. When Charlotte was halfway through filming series
    one of *Geordie Shore*, she came to meet me in the
    Metro Centre with her new friend Sophie. She wanted
    fifty pounds so she could buy an outfit for some event
    they were all going to. While we were shopping she
    told me, 'I've got a bit of a problem. I've kind of had
    sex on TV.' I remember standing outside Debenhams
    at the time. I wanted the ground to swallow me up.

6. Fame is a funny thing. It's not been nice to read when
    Charlotte's had negative comments written about her
    in the press, but she doesn't get wrapped up in it and
    she's good at being able to deal with it. I've even been
    trolled myself! Someone once trolled me for hanging
    my washing in my garden! Where do they expect me
    to hang my washing? I told them to fuck off.

7. I am so proud that Charlotte has done so many things that I didn't do at her age. I look back and wish I'd travelled to places and gone around the world. She's had so many great opportunities.

8. If I had to pick her worst ever boyfriend I would say it has to be . . . just using the initials 1) G 2) S 3) J . . . S nearly caused the whole family to stop speaking!

9. One of the things I'm most proud of is *Geordie Shore*. I think she made the show what it was and really took it to a brilliant level that maybe it never quite reached again after she left. She gave it her all when she was on the show. Charlotte is such a truly kind human being, and she continues to make me proud with every year that passes and everything she does.

10. I think people assume Charlotte puts on an act and she isn't the same as she is on TV. But we have such a funny time, she is so brilliant and emotional and crazy and we can laugh about the most stupid things.

11. A lot of people ask why Nathaniel doesn't have a big part in the fame element of Charlotte's life – but that's because he has Asperger's so he hates attention. Nathaniel has no interest whatsoever in being in the public eye. Charlotte offered to buy him something that was

nearly £1,000 but he still said, 'No!' We spend quality time with him as a family in the house – he's a very funny and intelligent young man and he really makes us all laugh.

2

My baby is . . .

not yet a reality because I am too busy with bad ex-boyfriends and being a boss business bitch!

It's so weird thinking that the last time I wrote a book about my life, which was my second one, *Brand New Me*, in 2017, I was still dating the idiot that is Stephen Bear. I mean, what the hell was I *doing*? But looking back now, I have decided I need to be philosophical about it all, because SURELY there's a reason why I was ever with him, and the two other not-ideal boyfriends who came along afterwards. I have to believe that life happens for a reason, and these tattooed-boys, who cared about how their hair looked more than they cared about me, came along to teach me something and prepare me for when I was going to finally meet *the one*.

I feel like I've learnt so much since 2017 and even though I've dated some dickheads I feel like they came into my life for a reason. They've taught me stuff and I've finally learnt to love myself in the process.

Lesson 1: You love being a boss and running a business

So first, Stephen Bear. Stephen Bear was absolutly the sort of person that I think of as a narcissist. I didn't even realise, there were people who existed like this! I remember I was madly into him at the time, but that's what narcissists do – they lure you in. A narcissist always showers you with affection to start with, so you fall for them. This way, they can distract you from their flaws and from the reality that they are a total dick who only cares about themselves!

I bumped into him in a restaurant a few years after we'd split, and it was fine – there weren't any plates being thrown or anything! We just said, 'Hello.' I remember looking at him and wondering what on earth I had ever seen in him. Apparently, he's now doing OnlyFans for a living, and I saw a photo of him recently and he looked like a right hillbilly, with crazy long hair.

One good thing that really stuck with me from my time with Stephen, was the realisation that I absolutely love channelling my creative ideas into a brand. I got my first taste of running an online brand when we were together. We set up a business called His and Hers, which was selling bags and hoodies and stuff. Well, when I say 'we', *I* actually put all the money into it and had the ideas, but we were together, so we said it was a joint thing. Of course, that all came back to bite me in the bum big time when we split, because things got nasty, and he threatened to sue me *and* my family. He kept sending messages to Dad, saying we owed him money when we never owed him a thing – he owed us in fact. So, we had to close the company just to enable us to sever all ties once and for all.

After dissolving the His and Hers brand I still had an entrepreneurial itch that needed scratching. And it was itchier than any thrush I'd ever had – so I needed to do something about it. I came to realise that I LOVE BEING A BUSINESS WOMAN! I have so many creative ideas and testing out the business with him just stoked the fire inside me! Back then we were just selling sweatshirts and mugs – but I got such a thirst for it. I loved having something that I could run and take charge of. So in 2019 I channelled all my ideas and excitement into Pepper Girls Club.

I came up with the name on a trip to South Africa when we were filming *The Charlotte Show*. We stayed in this really cool hotel called the Pepperclub and I remember thinking what a cute name it had. But obviously I couldn't just take that name as it was already established, so I just added the word 'Girls' in the middle of it. We started doing bags – I would come up with an idea I liked and then I'd spend hours ringing round places talking to people who ran factories, researching manufacturers and material and getting stuff sent to me as samples to test. We eventually found a manufacturer we really liked in Leicester. I did all the shipping and records. It's a real family thing – Mam helps me do all the packing and sending. We did it all on our own – no help, no investors, no designers. We've hired a family friend, Gabby, who deals with customer complaints and works part time. Our family has known Gabby and her sister, Holly, for a really long time – both of them are very close to our hearts. It's great having Gabby work for Pepper Girls Club because she's so organised and on time! Honestly, ever since she started working for the business it's been like an incredible love story. She's so good we've given her a pay rise already and she has the keys to open up. She's a real business attribute!

I'm not going to lie and make out I'm Victoria Beckham all of a sudden – I'm not a fashion designer. I am creative and I know what works and I have some ideas – but often I just scroll through Instagram trawling through other people's posts for inspiration. And what is it that they say – there's no such thing as an original idea? Well, I just dig very deep and I think about trends and I know what I like wearing and what works and suits different body types. If I'm being dead honest, most of the time I look at something and think, 'How could I upgrade that a little bit – a few tweaks here and there?' I don't like to do fast fashion, so we have just a few different collections of the bags a year – staple designs in different colourways. We pride ourselves on the quality of them and make sure they're like designer brands, but at affordable prices. We get so much amazing feedback too. People begging us to bring back certain colours and styles!

I like to morph it to whatever is going on in my life. We've now started doing baby changing bags because I realised there weren't any nice ones out there and I needed one! I wanted one with loads of different pockets and nooks and crannies to store stuff. The great thing, also, is that I have lots of amazing people following me on Instagram and I can ask them what they think, what they need and what they want designed. I would love to get to the point where I'm in my forties and I can sell it because it's so successful!

Lessons I've learnt from running a business

1. Lots of people who want to start a business are control freaks – you need to have a certain personality to take on all the stress and the pressure!
2. You can't do it without help though, which is why it's important to have a good team.
3. Work with people you really trust – for me that's me mam and dad. The second you start getting the correct

support is the second your business will grow to a whole new level.

4. Work out what your strengths are and what your weaknesses are – then find people who are good at the bits you're not so good at.

5. Make sure you have someone who is good with money (in my case, me dad) who can do your accounts for you, work out margins and make sure you make a profit. Also, there are all these extra things hiding like tax importation costs – things I haven't got a clue about!

6. You need to be driven. (I don't mean someone driving you around in a car . . . although it would be a nice sign you'd made it if you'd got yourself a chauffeur!)

7. You need to realise you will never switch off – you'll think about your business 24/7.

8. Don't expect to bring money in straight away. If you want to build a successful business, you need to keep that money and put it back into the company.

9. Don't be afraid to try something different. If your original vision didn't work, you might need to adapt it into something else. Don't be pig headed and stick to something that's not working.

10. Start small and build up.

11. Breathe.

12. Try to sleep.

13. DON'T PANIC!

14. Try not to fire yourself.

Lesson 2: When the world sees your relationship falling apart on TV – maybe it's time to move on

After Stephen I met Joshua Ritchie. We dated for nearly two years – most of which was documented on my MTV series *The Charlotte Show*. I loved doing that show, it was such a buzz to have my own reality programme that didn't involve me travelling around all over the world (we all know *The Charlotte Crosby Experience* wasn't me at my best). *The Charlotte Show* ran for three series from 2018 to 2019. Work was really good at that time because I was also still doing *Just Tattoo of Us*. When me and Stephen Bear split, MTV kindly replaced him with Joey Essex, who is a good mate. Joey could be a bit of a diva sometimes, and didn't really get his hands dirty, but he made me laugh. Whatever you might think about him – he always knew all his lines!

Josh and his family were a big part of *The Charlotte Show*, as were mine. And there's a scene where I am with his mam, Karen, and she's grilling me about my intentions with him and I'm saying he's the one. His mam even says she thinks I'm going to get married to Josh. She looks at the camera and says, 'I think next year they will get engaged.' And I'm also talking about wanting babies with him. Which is so weird to think about now.

There were some mad moments – like when we thought my house was haunted and had a guy called Les and his dog

Shay come over to exorcise the place! He said he could feel a presence of a man in a vest with black boots – I said he sounded either like me dad or a pirate! There was also the time when I broke my nose in a pool in South Africa because I headbutted Lauren when we were pushing her in. That was so scary. And there's a bit where I take me mam to see a doctor about getting some laser-tightening surgery on her vagina because she kept wetting herself when she was sneezing. The doctor showed us this MASSIVE probe that they have to insert into the fanny and I was shocked but Mam just smiled, 'Well, Gary's very big,' which made me want to vomit. I don't want to think about her and me dad having sex!

The only catch about *The Charlotte Show* was that it documented the good times *and* the bad times. And while it showed when me and Josh met and it was all going well – it also showed loads of our rows too. So, it's not fun to look back on as I don't really want to remember that time. There are so many scenes where we argue and bicker – and it's in front of our parents too. Also Josh is in pretty much every episode. So you can see where we had our issues and why the relationship was never going to work. We'd have rows, I'd get upset and he'd just walk off. I remember there was one scene where I went to surprise him in a club dressed as an elephant as a joke and he just stormed off because he thought I was trying to spy on him with his mates! I was in tears afterwards – in fact I was in tears most of the time in that relationship!

We got on for a while and did have fun when we were

together, but he was so immature. I really don't think he taught me much apart from not to trust young guys! For some stupid reason I decided to move away from my amazing big, huge, beautiful house and moved in with him in Bolton more than a hundred miles away. It was the biggest mistake of my life because I felt completely isolated away from my friends and family. I was convinced he cheated on me loads but he would never admit it, so I ended up feeling like I was going mad and was some psycho monster of a girlfriend – it was just constant gaslighting. He would be out doing stuff with other girls, and I would be driving myself crazy over it while he told me I was making stuff up. He played a good game at first, but by the end everyone in my circle knew I was right.

One time, when he was in Vegas, I made me mates stay on Vegas time so we could keep an eye on his Insta stories and see what he was up to! It was so blatant that he was up to no good – I'm not sure if he thought I wouldn't notice because of the time difference but I was sitting there at home on the sofa, with all me mates, sticks keeping our eyes open, playing demented detectives! This didn't just come out of nowhere – I'm not that much of a Miss Marple. I had people sending me messages in the days leading up to it, saying they were out there too and had seen him in nightclubs, with girls all over him, kissing their necks and stuff. And because he would always deny it, I just felt like I had to literally catch him in the act. Looking back on it now, I am so relieved I'm not in a relationship like that. So many sleepless nights, so many times doubting myself, so many moments where I questioned my sanity because he told me I was wrong and imagining things!

Jungle therapy

When things ended with Josh, I moved out of his house in Bolton and I had to live back with me mam and dad because I'd rented my house to another family. I wasn't prepared to kick the family out just because things had gone wrong on my end. But I was sad not to be back in the home I'd worked so hard for.

Then I got an amazing opportunity to be on *I'm A Celebrity Get Me Out Of Here* in Australia and thought I'd have loads of jobs afterwards so it wouldn't matter. I was so excited as I'd wanted to be on the show for years. I wanted to be in it so much that I used to Photoshop pictures of my head on the UK *I'm A Celebrity Get Me Out Of Here* line up. I couldn't believe it was actually happening. Australia wasn't quite the same, but it was a close second! Going to Australia was also a blessing because it meant being without my phone for a whole month. I was finding the break-up with Josh really hard. This way, I figured I wouldn't be tempted to call or text him. (Because you know how much you end up doing that after a break-up, even if you know the person is wrong, wrong,

wrong!) I actually think that show was the main reason I got over him. It was therapy.

Ironically, while I was in Australia, Kerry Katona wrote in her magazine column that I should turn to 'therapy' after my split from Joshua Ritchie, rather than surgery. She said she thought I looked better 'before surgery' and that, 'Her face looks like it's got stuck between two lift doors. She looks a bit like a cross-eyed fish.' As I was in the jungle I didn't see it, but Holly went for her and stuck up for me tweeting:

> What the hell is this!!? You are a mother
> to daughters!!!

My agent Kate was also fuming and complained to the magazine. Kerry apologised in the press afterwards and said she didn't intend to be 'mean' and was being 'tongue in cheek'. She also sent a big, long apology message in my DMs after I came out of the show. But writing this has just reminded me I haven't even replied!

Before we started filming, I said numerous times that I would never ever jump out of a helicopter and neither would I bungee jump. I think the producers didn't believe what I was saying. The first thing I was asked to do was BUNGEE jump out of a helicopter. I just couldn't do it and had to say, 'I'm a celebrity get me out of here.' I even wet myself a bit when I was asked to do it, I was so scared. I was sobbing, 'I can't do it. Oh, God. Why did I ever agree to come on the show? I don't want to do it. I've never wanted to not do something more in my life. Oh God!' Looking back I feel like I did embrace a bit of the challenge because I physically went up into the helicopter and that was the scariest thing I have ever done – I was at the edge with the bungee and that was bad enough!

No one knows this but I went for an interview to be on *Celebrity SAS: Who Dares Wins* not long after *I'm a Celeb* and this time I'd learnt my lesson. I really didn't want to do any challenges, I knew I couldn't jump out of a helicopter so when they asked me what I'd be up for I said no to that. They tried to push me by saying, 'But if it came to it and you were faced with having to jump out of the helicopter – you would, right?' I just shook my head matter of factly. I did such an awful interview they didn't ask me back.

It was so fun being in the jungle with a load of Australians. I bonded with so many great people there – especially comedian Dilruk Jayasinha. We had such a laugh. He hadn't ever seen anything I'd been on which I think was great because he had no preconceived notions of me. He always jokes that we're like the same person because he used to behave like me in his past. We had so many mad conversations and one night we were talking about life and death and where you go when you die. And then I said to him, 'By the way, do you know I can fanny fart on cue?'

He looked so shocked and was laughing his head off. 'What do you mean?!'

Then he saw me putting my hands down my pants and said, 'What the hell are you doing!?' and I replied, 'I've got to adjust my flaps first!

He was pissing himself laughing. 'How did we get from philosophy to fanny flaps so quickly?'

Later on he said, 'If you're like this when you're sober, what are you like when you're drunk?'

I love Dilruk so much.

Ryan Gallagher had been a contestant in *Married At First Sight Australia* and he was a lovely boy. We got on incredibly well and both developed feelings for one other. It was nice to have someone to have a flirt and cuddle with and I have nothing bad to say about him. But I was still very raw after the split from Josh and knew it wasn't wise getting into anything serious. The whole thing was a bit scary for me as it moved so fast. Being close to another boy reminded me how I'd just come out of a break-up and wasn't ready and I ended up blubbing loads on camera about it (well, this is me!). I'd come into the jungle because I thought I would have head space and truly find myself. Then I panicked because I didn't find me, instead I found another boy! I knew the last thing I should be doing was getting into another relationship. It was a pressured environment too – as I think the other campmates wanted us to be together somehow. In the end, we admitted we were in different stages in life – he was ready to settle and I wasn't – so we came to a mutual decision that we'd just cool it off. Once we were out, I tried to keep in touch as mates – I think I texted him about eight times – but he went quiet. I just knew I needed to have some time on my own where I could fall in love with myself again and not worry about anyone else.

While we were in the camp we were allowed to watch a clip of the news and that was the first time we heard about COVID. We were watching all these reports of this outbreak in China and were thinking, 'Oh God, I wonder what's going on over there then?' We thought it was a bit of pointless news to show us because we didn't realise it was going to affect us. Little did we know it was going to be a global pandemic! That memory will always stay with me.

Despite meeting some great people, I wouldn't rush to do a show like that again though – I was just so hungry!

When I got home from Australia I had to move in with Mam and Dad again! I was about to turn thirty and I was back in the family home. Single. I recall sitting in my little bedroom, all the furniture and belongings I had stuffed into one place, feeling incredibly sorry for myself and comparing my life to everyone else's. People were getting engaged, buying their own homes, having kids, moving on with their lives . . . and I was back where I began.

3

My baby is . . .

hiding behind closed doors while
I cough and splutter A LOT

Thankfully, it turned out my thirties were not so tough after all. Not long after I'd been sitting there feeling sorry for myself the family that were renting my place moved out meaning I could finally go back home. And then I got with a boyfriend who was unlike any of the others I had ever met. In other words – he was normal. He was a nice human being. He also taught me something I had never known before – RESPECT.

I met Liam Beaumont quite randomly, on a night out in Dubai, where he was living, in early 2020. Liam was completely different to Joshua and Stephen – and, being with him DID teach me loads of good stuff about relationships. The first lesson he taught me was that not all boys are absolute arseholes. Which then, in turn, made me a much calmer and nicer girlfriend because I wasn't paranoid all the time.

At first, I thought it was just a holiday romance – and looking back that was probably what it was meant to be all along – but COVID happened about a month into us meeting which threw us more permanently together and I think we probably rushed into things. Liam had nowhere to go when he came back from Dubai – he couldn't move back in with his mam, because his brothers were living there – so he ended up moving into mine. Liam had a good job, as a producer and videographer (which turned out quite handy for my social media in lockdown!). I really liked him, he was funny, kind and I loved how many tattoos he had – but deep down I knew he wasn't the love of my life. But because it was lockdown, I didn't want to kick him out on the street. So, I convinced myself we could make it work. Also, I'm not the type of person who likes being on their own so, probably quite selfishly, I wanted him as company. I'm sure lockdown forced a lot of people into situations they didn't want to be in. I doubt I'm the only one!

When COVID hit, all my work dried up, and I was stuck at home twiddling my thumbs. (That's a lie, I have never twiddled my thumbs. Who even does that? Surely that would be painful!) But I was definitely bored and also thinking this was possibly the end of my TV career. So I found myself another way to keep busy.

Given how much I loved Pepper Girls Club, I decided to launch ANOTHER BUSINESS – an interiors one called Naked Lane Interiors. I was bored, and I always need to be doing something – plus I LOVED doing up my house and coming up with different designs and ideas for the rooms. And no one else from reality shows like me seemed to be doing it – there were lots of people doing little hacks and tidying fixes, but not selling actual furniture. And as it was lockdown everyone seemed to be talking about their houses and wanting to redo them because they were stuck inside the whole time and needed to suddenly use their lounge as an office and their bedroom as a gym.

The thing is, you must spend a lot of money to start with as you have to buy the stock and then also find somewhere to store it. And you never quite know what's going to sell and what isn't, you're just trusting your instinct at first. But if no one buys the pieces, you're stuck with them!

So I did loads of research again. I found these amazing wood craftsmen in England who were making lovely pieces out of reclaimed timber – so I stocked up on a load of recycled wood pieces from them. I also partnered with an Irish artist who'd done all the prints I had in my house and her prints did really well. I loved the stories from both the woodsmen and the artist as they were their own home-grown businesses so I felt like I was helping to support local talent. We did get a few other bits that were wholesale, and some imported from India – like these gorgeous mosaic trays – but tried to keep most from the UK. The business started doing really well but then I got carried away. I ordered a big shipment of furniture, which I was convinced was going to fly. I spent about forty grand in total on these massive items. I had to price them at a decent figure to make any money on them, and I think they were just the wrong price bracket for my type of customer in the end. All in all, it was a big learning curve because we were STUCK WITH ALL THESE MASSIVE TABLES AND WARDROBES!

Another REALLY annoying thing that happened was that I got a letter from the Advertising Standards Authority accusing me of not declaring I was being paid to advertise for Pepper Girls Club and Naked Lane Interiors. I was suddenly on a 'name and shame' naughty list! I challenged their ruling because I'd been completely transparent about them being my own companies; I wasn't personally getting any money as I was putting everything back into the businesses. Apparently, I didn't make it blatant enough, which then meant I had to write 'this is my own business by the way' on nearly every single post! THEN I got shouted at because I didn't put #AD on all the posts I did for In The Style. I admit that *was* my fault. I just forgot, because when I started designing clothing ranges with Adam and Jamie it was way before you had all these rules. But I said sorry for that one. AND THEN I got another telling-off because I tagged a nail brand when I got my nails done – which I had PAID for! It was not an advertisement. It was not a gift! But yes, I shouted the girl out because she was amazing. I think most people they catch out don't pay for things. So when I showed them all the receipts, they didn't seem to know what to do.

But they say 'everything happens for a reason', and another favourite of mine is that you have to 'fail forward' so all of this has taught me some really valuable lessons about what not to do! I'm pleased to report that the business is still going strong.

Your specialist subject is . . . whales!

Thankfully I was wrong about no more TV work because in 2020 I got the phone call of all phone calls. The request I never thought would ever come. I was invited to be on . . . wait for it . . . do not adjust your TV sets . . . *Mastermind*. Admittedly it was the celebrity version that went out over Christmas, but it was still ridiculously difficult and I took the whole thing incredibly seriously. With the lockdown I hadn't been on TV for ages, so when Kate got the request one day she said, 'I think this could be a good show for you to do.'

So I thought, 'Why not? I'll give it my best shot.' I decided I'd play to raise money for The Ectopic Pregnancy Trust, a charity very close to my heart after my ectopic pregnancy in 2016.

The thing is, I'd hardly ever watched *Mastermind*, so I wasn't exactly prepared for what I was letting myself in for. I didn't know how hard it was. I had to let them know what my specialist subject would be, so me, being me, picked the hardest subject imaginable. Why on earth did I decide I would speak about whales, dolphins and porpoises? I mean yes, I love them and am a bit obsessed with them – but I AM NOT A MARINE BIOLOGIST! I didn't realise you could pick TV shows or films and stuff. I was on the show with Omid Djalili, Dr Zoe Williams (the doctor on *This Morning*), and former England rugby player James Haskell. When I got there, James Haskell had chosen Harry Potter and I thought, 'WHY HAVE I CHOSEN SEA LIFE?!!' I chose it because they're my favourite animals, right? But I didn't realise you could choose Harry Potter! God, why didn't I go for something easy like that?! My Little Pony!?

James Haskell chose all the Harry Potter films, so that's where all the questions came from. You'd think that would be easier, but the questions were actually really bizarre. A bit like they'd been for TOWIE's Lydia Bright – back in 2018 she picked *Friends* and I thought that would have been easy too, but one of her questions was, 'What drink did Gunther make Rachel in episode five, series three?' I mean WHAT THE HELL!!?? How on earth would you ever remember that?

I studied whales from back to front. Kate was on the phone to me three times a week testing my knowledge. She was giving me mock tests and I was doing so well. But when it came to the show, they asked the questions in a really weird way that made it so much harder than it needed to be. And I knew so much information on whales, dolphins and porpoises – I was literally a brainbox on them by the end of my revision. I studied for a full month, day in day out. But when they asked the questions, it just threw me right off. Even Kate said afterwards they seemed to make it trickier.

The host, John Humphreys, asked me at one point how I managed to rake in over 7 million followers on my official Instagram account. I replied back, 'Do you know what, John, I ask myself this all the time.' I then said, 'It's obviously not for the dolphin facts. I don't know them clearly.' Then he asked me about my tattoos, and I told him, 'I won't show the one on my thigh, John, it's a little high up.'

Everyone seemed to find it hilarious that I was on the show.

One tweeted:

Was not expecting Charlotte Crosby to choose
Whales, Dolphins and Porpoises as her subject
#CelebrityMastermind.

A second wrote:

Things you thought you'd never see – Charlotte
Crosby on Mastermind #celebrityMasterMind,' 😆.

One of my favourites was:

> Putting Charlotte Crosby on Mastermind is probably
> like asking a cabbage to fix a nuclear reactor.

Another tweeted:

> If Charlotte Crosby wins #celebrityMasterMind
> I am officially done with 2020.

And my favourite one of all:

> Charlotte Crosby's performance on Mastermind was
> absolute inspiration. Not because she was any good,
> but because she was the most 'real' contestant I've
> ever seen.

I don't know about being 'real', mind you. When I watched it back, I thought I looked like one of the people from the Dolmio adverts! The light on my face was really bright and I'd chosen this pink lipstick that was really glossy and made my lips look even bigger than they were. It was quite a scary sight. I didn't look like a real human.

You will be impressed to know that I still know some of the facts now – they're stuck in my head. One of the questions they asked was about a killer whale and that was a trick question. Because actually the killer whale is not a whale, it's part of the dolphin family. I got that one right! I still know the sperm whale has the largest brain on earth. And it sleeps horizontally. And it is the longest living mammal on the planet. That's three good facts! There are two main types of whales – there's baleen whales and toothed whales. I think it's to do with what they eat – baleen whales have baleen plates in their mouths that allow them to eat krill and plankton, while toothed whales, like the sperm whale, have teeth that they use for hunting fish and other larger sea creatures. But I didn't manage to get any of this into my answers at all! Because they didn't ask me about these facts!

So I really struggled with the specialist round and only got two right. But during the second round, I got four of the general knowledge questions right and couldn't help but jump around cheering! Sadly, I still came last!

When I was interviewed afterwards, I was saying, 'I know so much! I haven't had a chance to show my knowledge!!' I was absolutely furious! Thank God those lights went down because a tear nearly came out my eye because I was that frustrated! I just didn't understand! I'd even worn my lucky whale necklace – it had a whale's tail on. I felt like ripping it off and throwing it on a fire, melting it down and selling it. I did hours upon hours of revision. I could tell you the maximum weight of blue whale, male and female. But why didn't that question come up?!

*   *   *

My love for whales hasn't been for nothing though. Just before I went out to Australia for *I'm a Celebrity Get Me Out of Here*, I was proud to support a campaign for PETA against SeaWorld – trying to stop them from keeping whales and dolphins confined in cramped concrete tanks at amusement parks. Some of the ways they hold these beautiful creatures are so cruel. So, I took part in a stunt where I was 'trapped' inside this tank of water and couldn't get out. It was meant to make people realise even more how awful and massively cruel it is – how claustrophobic it is being in such a small space.

When I got in the water I couldn't believe how HOT it was! There was no way I could be floating around in there! It had taken hours to get all that water in the tank, but in the end they had to get a load of it out and top it up with cold water before I could get in it.

But it was all for a good cause. Animals will keep on living and dying in misery as long as people support places like Sea-World. I love entertaining people, but animals aren't given a choice and that's abuse. Wild animals, especially ones the size of whales, should be kept in their natural environment and not in tanks. I feel that a lot of people don't understand how cruel it is. I hoped that when people were educated on that it might change their minds about ever stepping in a park again.

The name's Andre, Peter Andre

Another show I filmed at the end of 2020 was *The Celebrity Circle* on Channel 4. It was such a fun job and really different. I was such a huge fan of *The Circle*. I just love TV, I'm one of those people who has seen every single reality show. Everyone's like, 'Are you watching *Selling Sunset*? Are you watching this?' I'm like, 'Yeah, I've watched them all.' I am obsessed with TV. You know when you meet people and they're like, 'I just don't watch TV.' I'm like, 'Why?' How could you not watch TV? It's my favourite thing to do. When I watched the very first series of *The Circle*, I just thought it was an amazing concept. And the fact you could be anyone. The idea is that you're all in this block of flats communicating with each other on social media, but no one knows who's real and who's not. It's like the MTV show *Catfish*, but you're watching that unfold and you know the actual character. I just always thought I would love to do that show if they ever did the celebrity version.

So, I got to catfish and pretend I was someone else. I went in pretending I was Peter Andre. I wasn't always going to be him – the person I originally wanted to be was Eamonn Holmes but I don't think his agent liked the idea (I don't know why!) so I had to change my mind. Then it was going to be Keith Lemon who I love, but the show producers suggested Peter and I thought that would be really funny.

47

I've met Peter Andre a couple of times and I really like him – I mean, who doesn't like Peter Andre? He's won Dad of the Year about seventy-five years in a row. How can you not like Dad of the Year? He's such a nice guy. I took his autobiography in there with me for research and because it was quite boring sitting in the room on your own I ended up reading the whole thing. I cried loads because there was some really sad stuff about him losing his brother.

My game plan in there was just to try and be friends with everyone. Pete is very positive, you'd know if someone was feeling down, he'd be the one to cheer them up. He's good with his words, he's a bit of a shoulder to cry on. I think he's a big morale booster, isn't he? So I thought that's what I want to try and be. I didn't think I could cause mischief as Peter Andre, because people were going to suspect something was off. He's not a mischief maker. When I came out of the show Peter Andre reached out and said he really enjoyed it and it was so funny!

The show was supporting Stand Up To Cancer – and I remember being asked why I wanted to do it. I said, 'Everyone's been affected by cancer at some point, sadly. It's just such an awful disease that seems to be everywhere. It's so common. My grandad died two years ago from prostate cancer.' At the time that was the only person in my family who'd been affected by it . . . little did I know that a year after the show came out our family would be affected by it in an even bigger way. I was so glad I could support such an important charity.

A short story about isolation . . .

Not long after *The Circle* I was booked to go on an exciting radio tour to promote my podcast with Nova who have a radio station in Australia, but typical me ended up testing positive for COVID, and being kept in a security hospital for TWENTY-TWO DAYS. I was in there so long I got dumped from the tour!

Here's how these hideous events unfolded . . .

When I did a COVID test to travel to Australia it was negative, but just as I landed, I was beginning to feeling a bit wheezy, like I had some sort of chest infection. I sometimes get one on a long flight, so I just put it down to that. I can't even speak because my cough gets so bad – I think it's the air conditioning. So, when I was on the plane and the cough started again and I was spluttering all over the other passengers, I simply thought, 'Oh no, it's happening again.' Never in my wildest dreams did I think it was COVID. Besides, I had to go straight to a quarantine hotel before I could enter the country properly anyway.

On my way to the COVID quarantine hotel, I was dreading it. I've never been so nervous in my whole entire life – mainly because I don't like being alone. I hate it! I was thinking, 'How am I going to do this? I'm going to be alone for so long!' Also, in the lead-up to going there I had been researching 'quarantine hotels' and they were awful. You would be lucky even if you had a window to open. I wasn't looking forward to it AT ALL. This was not helped by scrolling Instagram and seeing *Strictly Come Dancing*'s Dianne Buswell stuck in one– she looked miserable and it looked horrendous. When I arrived it was like something out of the apocalypse – the army were everywhere, people carrying guns, walking around in hazmat suits, the full PPE uniform. It was terrifying.

Before I could get my key to my room, I had to sign all these forms giving away my life story and every minute detail of anywhere and everywhere I had been, sniffed, touched, licked and coughed on before arrival. I was told a person would then come and give me the key. After a while a man came over. He slid this key across the table, smiled and said, 'It's your lucky day!' I was confused. 'What? What? What does this *mean?*' Immediately I got marched up by the army man with a gun, all the way up to my floor. I walked into the room and I gasped. I'd only been given a suite with two balconies hadn't I?! Wow. I wanted to hug the man with the gun, but obviously that was not allowed! Oh my God! I have won the lottery! This is going to be amazing! I can easily do this! I have a balcony! I was so happy at this point, thinking, 'This is going to be a BREEZE!' But as I went to bed that night, the coughing started to get really bad. I rang downstairs and said politely, 'Hello, can I have some honey and water please? Honey and lemon would be amazing if possible – I've got a terribly sore throat.' I was still blissfully unaware that it could ever be COVID and didn't have a clue that ringing them up would be setting off serious alarm bells. Clearly, as soon as I'd said those words there was panic stations going on all around me in the hotel – 'Code red! Code red! Someone's got COVID!'

I was so adamant that I didn't have it though and was being really calm and measured, 'Honestly, don't worry it's not COVID. I get a chest infection every time I fly on a long-haul flight. There is absolutely no chance this is COVID. I just need some amoxicillin, so if you can get me a doctor that would be great.'

In the end, because I was so sure of myself, they said, 'Well, let's see how you go. We have to do a COVID test on day three anyway.'

So I thought, 'Fine, it won't be COVID and the sore throat will be gone by then.'

Two days go by, they give me my hot water, lemon and honey . . . and my throat keeps getting worse. Meanwhile, there were all these rules you had to abide by in the place and I was always forgetting and then having to correct myself. If there was a knock at the door then you were supposed to wait thirty seconds after the knock to open it but sometimes I would forget and nearly open it too quickly. You were also supposed to have your mask on when anyone came in so I was always rushing to put mine on.

On the third day, I had to do the COVID test. I was feeling awful by this point. When I woke up, I could hardly open my eyes, I was so tired and my cough was wild. But I did the test and went back to bed to wait for them to call with the results. Then the doctor rang and spoke to me in this really matter-of-fact voice 'Hi, Miss Crosby, this is the doctor. We've got your results back from the COVID test.'

I interrupted him before he could finish, I was so cocky and sure I didn't have it: 'It's not COVID is it, so I wonder what it could be because I still feel pretty bad.'

There was a dramatic pause. 'It is in fact COVID, yes.'

I was in shock.

'Anyway,' he continued really forcefully, 'we're going to need you to leave your room straight away. Do not pick up any of your belongings. Everything needs to be fumigated. You're going to be escorted now to a hospital hotel.'

Oh my fucking God. This would only happen to me when I've come to the other side of the world to do a tour. The doctor continued, 'So now your quarantine will need to restart.'

I was thinking to myself, 'I've already been here for four days – and that's all wiped off and it has to start again from zero. This is like some really shit game show.' The next thing I knew, there was an army of people in full PPE, all ready to take me. I even got a police escort. I got put in an ambulance and there was a police car driving in front and behind us making sure we got safely to the next hotel,

I arrived at the hospital hotel and looked at the place. It was nothing like my previous life of luxury and I thought, 'Oh, this is just AWFUL!' Mind you, even if I'd had a swanky balcony, I'd never have had the energy to stand on it because the following ten days were HELL. I felt so ill. I wouldn't wish it on my worst enemy. My symptoms were wild – every day there was something different. One day my eyes were so dry that I couldn't open them, and I had to have a hot flannel over my face. Wow, and the aches and pains! Oh my God – my back was in agony. I also had constant diarrhoea and lost my sense of taste for about three days; after that I lost my sense of smell for two days and I was feeling like this for ten days. I know the times because I was logging it all. I've got a thing with logging stuff so I can keep track of what's happening to me. I got it really bad. I just couldn't believe how bad it had hit me. But it was probably because it was the first time I'd had it.

Also, I was having to have daily checks. You know when you're really ill you can barely even get out of bed? Well, this didn't seem to be an issue because the doctors had me out of bed three times a day. One minute it was to do blood pressure, the next to check blood oxygen, then swabs. And then they were constantly ringing the room because I was having to do about a million questionnaires. So, they would ring and make me go through this form which was on the other side of the room. I'd be sat on the phone on this uncomfortable chair feeling so awful while they asked me 5,000 questions about where I'd been on this day and that day and who I'd been in contact with.

I remember sitting watching TV and there was this news flash – 'Breaking news, breaking news. The Delta variant has entered Australia!'

I was still convinced I'd be able to do the tour though! I thought, 'I'm still going to be fine because I'll get out in a few days and maybe they will wait for me?'

I was blissfully convinced it would still happen. I thought they'd be calling me to start rehearsals over Zoom any time soon. But meanwhile the whole of Sydney was going into lockdown. I'd been telling myself to try to keep strong and fit so I was prepped and ready – even though I'd been ill, towards the end I'd dragged myself out of bed because I knew I had to get myself ready for the tour as I was so weak. I'd been on the exercise bike, doing mini workouts, I'd got myself a little routine. But I was so wired and delusional that I'd lost track of time and hadn't realised it was getting ridiculously close to the tour dates so there was really no way I'd be able to do them.

Then my Australian agent, Shane, rang me, 'Sorry, Charlotte, but we've cancelled the tour and appearances.' I was mortified. I was gutted. Honest to God, that feeling. I'd already spent over seventeen days in quarantine alone by this point. And the only reason I was out in Australia was to do this tour. So the feeling that I got when I found out that I wasn't even going to be doing it – was devastating. Honestly, I think I actually had a bit of a mental breakdown in the room. My earth came shattering down. I sat on the bed going, 'ARGGG-HHHHHH!!!' and rocking back and forth like a mad person.

And I still couldn't even go home because I wasn't allowed out until I tested negative. I still tested positive for days after that. I was still testing positive TWENTY-TWO days after I'd got to the hotel. I'd had the tour ripped away from me, and then, when I was finally allowed to go back to England, I had to isolate again for God knows how many days. WHAT AN ABSOLUTE DISASTER!

Anyway, one upside is that during those weeks in quarantine I'd become VERY accustomed to my own company. I was learning to cope with being single and on my own. So once I was home I felt like I could cope with anything that was thrown at me.

I don't think Liam and I were best suited in the end. We had such a fun time, but I think Liam just wanted to be back in Dubai living it up and partying, whereas I wanted to settle down in Sunderland. One of the issues was that I knew he didn't want kids and I DESPERATELY DID! (I had this with a lot of my boyfriends if I'm honest – one mention of the word BABIES and they would practically do a poo in their pants.)

In the end, he just walked out of the house saying, 'I don't think I'll ever make you happy.' And I didn't stop him. I was too cowardly to finish it myself, but when he did it for me, I knew it was for the best. I was content with the prospect of life as a single person. He's now back in Dubai living his best life.

I have no bad feelings or negative words to say about that relationship. It was so positive and taught me so many lessons and I am nothing but grateful for it. It's almost like it paved the way for me being ready to meet my proper boyfriend,

Jake Ankers. I believe that I needed to have a sensible, mature relationship that could end on good terms with an ex I didn't absolutely hate. So, no resentment, no nastiness, it just wasn't meant to be. It is actually mind-blowing to have that as a break-up experience! Ultimately Liam taught me that you can have a relationship where you aren't constantly cheated on, made to feel paranoid, or made to feel like a psychopath!

There's a saying that people come into your life for 'a reason, a season or a lifetime'. And with Liam there was definitely a 'reason'. Now it was time to manifest the man who was going to be my 'lifetime' . . .

4

My baby is . . .

just around the corner because I am about
to meet Jake Ankers — the love of my life
and my ONE AND ONLY!

After Liam, I decided to throw myself into singledom. It was
the first time in my life that I had ever actually been content and happy to be by myself. And I genuinely had Liam
to thank for a lot of that, as he'd made me feel secure and
confident in myself. I was determined that, this time round,
I was going to save myself for a decent human. I had learnt
that I was worth more than a dickhead boy and I promised
myself I wouldn't waste any more time on wrong 'uns.

I was single for just over three months. I threw myself
into exercise – I was running, walking or going to the gym

between two and four times a day and I was eating really healthily. I wasn't going out and I was hardly drinking – I was just dead focused on me and being my best self. I've always really enjoyed fitness and lockdown got me back into it – I'd go on twelve-hour walks and thrive on being outside in nature. It made me feel better both inside and out, mentally as well as physically, and I was on such good form. I honestly didn't think about guys for ages but then, after a while, I started feeling horny all the time. And there's only so much porn you can watch! No sex for months. No talking to any boys. I was starting to feel desperate for a flirt. So, I texted Lauren, my best friend from school. 'It would be nice to have a little flirt with someone. I quite fancy having a bit of texting and a kiss.'

That's all she needed to get her going as a dating expert on an extravaganza! She started sending me Instagram profiles of people she thought I might like. I scrolled through a few of them who I didn't fancy at all, and then I came across a guy called Jake. Lauren said, 'This is a good one! We've actually met him before – New Year's Eve in 2015.' I remembered that night quite vividly because it was in the height of *Geordie Shore* and it was a mad old crazy time. I think he was the promoter of the nightclub we were at in Manchester. But I had so much going on back then, I didn't notice him in that way. I looked at his photo and he looked really smiley and handsome. (I also noticed he had big ears which I thought were really cute in a Dumbo-the-elephant kind of way.)

I'd had enough time on my own by now to decide on a strict

checklist for any future relationship and one of those was that the guy had to have his own money and own business. I wanted someone with ambition who wasn't going to just be with me because of what I could offer him. Jake was clearly doing well for himself because Lauren pointed out that he had loads of businesses tagged under his profile. So, we checked them all out – basically turning into the FBI at this point. One of his businesses is an executive driving business with a fleet of cars which seemed very fancy. He just seemed amazing. Determined, ambitious, driven, successful and sorted. He was the perfect match for me – was he too good to be true?!

Charlotte's brand new boyfriend criteria checklist

1. Has his own stuff going on – a proper job (or jobs).
2. Ambitious and driven.
3. Ready for things like marriage . . .
4. . . . and babies.
5. Loyal.
6. Faithful.
7. Sweet.
8. Kind.
9. Funny.
10. Doesn't want to be famous.
11. And most important of all – have good morals.

Isn't it funny that there was nothing about looks on here at all? What makes men most attractive is the kind of person they are. I have come to the conclusion that most pretty boys are narcissists who are more in love with themselves than anyone else.

I kept looking at Jake's profile and getting excited at how perfect he seemed.

Lauren said, 'Come on then! Why don't you send him a DM?'

'NO! Never in a million years would I do that.'

'Why not? What have you got to lose?'

I decided I would just 'like' a couple of Jake's photos instead of messaging him. I honestly didn't think that he'd see them – certainly not as fast as he did! I did a couple of 'likes' at 7pm and by 7.06pm he'd slid into my DMs. It was so FAST! And he sent me the EYES emoji. Which meant he was watching me! After that we started sending silly things back and forth. He didn't believe it was me at first, he thought it was my agent running my Instagram! I mean, no offence to Kate, but I could never imagine her going back and forth with a guy like Jake doing kisses and eyes emojis!! Ha ha, the thought of that really makes me laugh!

I had a spider on my curtain so obviously I started telling him about that which, for some reason, he took to mean I was round the corner from him in Manchester. He then asked where I was based, and I told him I was in Sunderland. I remembered that I'd been asked by me mate to go to an event the following evening for a sofa company called Sofa Club. 'Ah, but I am in Manchester tomorrow!' I announced. It was like it was all matching up perfectly!

Jake replied, 'I'd love to pick you up afterwards and take you for some food and maybe a nice date.'

I was thinking to myself, 'I don't think anyone's *ever* taken us on a proper date!'

Then, after asking for my number seven hundred times (I was playing hard to get to start with), he left me a voice note. And honest to God, his voice was SO SEXY. I mean, I had been single for a while now, so already the slightest thing was going to tip me over the edge. He drooled, 'You just let me know what time you arrive at the hotel. I've got a driver on all night and I can pick you up and take you to your event and make sure you get back to your hotel safely.'

And I was thinking, 'Oh my God, this is like *Fifty Shades of Grey*!' – because you know how he's always got the driver taking whatever-her-name-is around, in between all the kinky sex? I'm thinking, I HAVE MY OWN MR GREY! I don't deserve a driver! This doesn't happen to me! I normally just neck on in a nightclub and then I'm stuck with them. But this was like a whole new realm, a world I'd never been in before.

When I got to the event (I was wearing a little green dress) I stood looking around waiting for him to arrive – while pretending I was doing the total opposite. As soon as I saw him walk through the door my heart jumped. He looked SO hot and sexy, dressed head to toe in black (turns out he'd just been to a football match). He sauntered over to the bar, smiling, shaking hands with people, chatting to literally EVERYONE he met. He knew more people there than I did. He just had this aura about him and was unlike any other bloke I'd met. I thought, 'Wow this is quite cool,' because normally, if someone had come to meet me at an event, it was always a bit awkward to start with because I knew it was going to be me having to look after them. But I didn't have to do anything! And then he came over with two bottles of champagne. As you know, I don't really like champagne, so I just said, 'Can't we just have Jägerbombs?'

I was a little bit nervous at first, but he made the conversation feel easy. We had a few drinks and then we had a kiss in the disabled toilet! I asked him where the loo was and he walked me down there, so I dragged him in with me and we snogged. It was intense and it was GOOD. After that we went out with the owner of Sofa Club and his wife, who is my friend. We had more drinks, and then we went back to Jake's and . . . let's just say we had a passionate night!

This was on 15th September 2021. Jake had to go to work the next day but we just didn't want to leave each other. From then on, we were inseparable. Because we lived in different cities, we started having the chat about how serious we were pretty early on. I think by day two, we'd already discussed being boyfriend and girlfriend! I asked him if he'd like to have kids one day and he said, 'Yes, of course.' It was such a refreshing feeling as I'd never been able to be that direct with boys before – they'd practically run out of the door to jump off the nearest cliff. Jake was like no one I'd ever come across in my life. The biggest romantic I'd ever met – he was so generous. He was kind and he was very confident. Very suave. I loved his cheeky smile. Everything about him was perfect.

It turned out Jake is literally the boy version of me. He has got so much love to give and, exactly like me, all he wants is to be loved just as much in return. He wants to fall in love with someone and build an amazing future with them. It makes me cry even just writing these words now. But he wants EXACTLY what I want in life – it's like we are both the same person. Like me, he's been in relationships where he has constantly been hurt. I've been with some awful, awful people who have treated me badly and cheated on me and he's had the same. I don't know how anyone could ever cheat on Jake. But some of the stories he's told me about his exes are just horrendous. In fact, I would go so far as to say he's had it worse than me – and who'd have thought *that* would be possible when it came to being unlucky in love? It's meant to be, because we both cry all the time. We just find ourselves stuck together sobbing over everything because we are so full of emotions. We'll start talking about our future and babies and then we need a box of tissues because we're blubbing so much.

He is just the best person who's ever walked this earth.

And he literally swept me off my feet.

I told some of me mates, but we kept it very secret from

the press. I didn't even tell me mam for ages! Obviously, Lauren was one of the first I confided in, because she was the one who set us up. She *loved it* and kept saying things like, 'Oh my God, I hope this turns into something!' Sophie joked that she was angry because she wanted me to be single with her!

Jake's first meeting with Mam wasn't how I'd planned it at all. I wanted it to be at a nice fancy restaurant so they could have a proper chat and get to know each other. But Jake decided to come to surprise me after one of my live shows when I was on tour (more on that in a minute). It was really nice, but everyone was drunk and Mam was dead tired. Then after that he met her at the house and now they're insepa-rable. They are so close, it's a joke. They just love going out and getting drunk. And obviously for most of that time I've been pregnant so I can't get involved, but the pair of them are constantly hanging out, going to restaurants, and shopping together. Always pissed! She absolutely loves him. You could not have a bad word said against him in her company, because she worships the ground he walks on.

Me dad is the same. He and Jake are both football crazy, so they had a bond pretty instantly. And there was one time, when they drove all the way to Southampton from Sunderland to watch a match, and the car broke down on the motorway. The fastest they could drive it after that was fifty miles an hour. So, what should have been a five-hour journey took them, like, nearly seven hours, there and back. And afterwards they both said it was the best seven hours of their lives because they didn't come up for air! They just talked about football the whole way.

My brother Nathaniel usually takes a little longer to warm to someone because people often don't know how to deal with him because of his autism (as you know, he has Asperger's). They don't always know how to talk to him and end up being a bit too forceful and trying too hard. But with Jake it was just dead natural and warm, and there has never needed to be too much effort required. Nathaniel is just really relaxed with him.

I also feel so blessed that I've got another family in my life too with Jake's mam and brother. I absolutely love his younger brother Reece. He's got the same characteristics as Jake – very kind and polite and warm. Just a lovely, lovely man with lots of charisma. The three of us have this nice relationship where we always take the piss out of each other – we've got a little family group chat on WhatsApp. Their mam, Natalie, is completely adorable too – as soon as we met I knew we'd get on – she's so easy to be with and nothing feels like hard work around her, the conversation always flows. We can even sit in silence and feel so comfortable and natural (not that I'm one for sitting quietly, mind). Jake doesn't speak to his dad much, but Natalie's partner, Chris, is the loveliest man and he's been like a dad to Jake and Reece. He really does a lot for them. Chris has helped shape Jake and made him want to be a brilliant dad himself.

'One Night with Charlotte' —
a short moment to remember my live tour

At the same time as I was getting to know Jake, I was getting ready for my live tour: 'One Night with Charlotte'.

We'd first had the idea back in 2019 and tried it one night in Liverpool in a club called Camp and Furnace. It went so well and was so much fun and we knew we wanted to take it on the road. So we did a deal with Live Nation who were adamant they could make it would work in bigger venues.

But then lockdown happened, so we had to wait until people were allowed to sit next to each other again. Once we were allowed, I was really apprehensive though, because two years had passed since the first show, and I wasn't really doing all that much in the public eye; I'd only been on telly a few times since then. If no one had heard from me, or seen me, for so long, were people going to even care? I panicked that no one would want to come! For the first time I thought I might have to admit defeat and that it was over for me. I was starting to accept that my time was up and that I would perhaps need to just focus on my businesses instead. It was going to happen one day – and maybe this was it. It had been a good ride but perhaps it was time to say goodbye . . .

But the tour was still planned to go ahead, and Live Nation wanted me to start advertising tickets. I was shitting myself that it was going to be a big flop. My only saving grace was that the capacity had halved in venues because people still couldn't be that close together. This meant I felt a bit less pressure! We had about 8,000 tickets to sell in total, I took a deep breath, posted it on my socials and waited . . . I was expecting tumbleweed and silence but I sold over 4,000 in the first few days. I was in shock – PEOPLE STILL CARED!!

Newcastle was the hardest to sell. Everyone else thought that it would be my biggest audience, but I knew it wouldn't. People see me in Newcastle all the time and I think they're sick to death of me! They HATE everyone from *Geordie Shore* too. They're just fed up of the sight of us. I was convinced the London dates would fail – but they were a sell-out. I was bowled over – there was me thinking no one would come and no one would be interested. But there were over a thousand people there, people were having to be taken away in ambulances because it got so crazy – one girl split her head open falling off a chair! It was WILD. People were in the aisles doing the worm – everyone was so pissed out of their heads.

The whole concept of the show was my idea – I'm actually quite creative you know! Sophie was in it with me, and we filmed some stuff beforehand. We made it look like we were getting ready for the show backstage and that I was taking ages, Sophie was banging on the door until she ended up just getting fed up and going on stage. We played this at the beginning and then Sophie came on stage without me and said her opening line, 'Well, well, well. Charlotte is late again. I suppose we're going to have to turn this into the Sophie Kasaei show.' Then the graphics changed on the board and it turned into 'The Sophie Kasaei Show' – and that was my cue to come on and say, 'Oh no, no, no! This is not happening!' and everyone cheered. Then we'd do a bit of a chat on stage and then introduce me mam who was stood in her own booth on the side as 'DJ Mam'. We just had loads of funny stupid songs. I would ask her to play something she made last week and it would be really shit, like cows mooing, and so I would tell her to stop because it was too awful. The crowd loved it!

It was a wild party night with everyone drinking all the time. We had this pop-up bar with a light-up frame set up at the front called 'Bijoux', which was obviously a reference to the club we always went to in *Geordie Shore*. It was like having a VIP area right at the front of the stage. Sophie was the host in Bijoux – or Nathan if he was doing the show with me instead of her. I explained at the beginning of the show that everyone in the audience would get the chance to win a spot inside Bijoux, and if you did, you'd get your drinks free all night. Every show everyone got a goody bag too so there was another chance to win by someone having a gold star for them and their mate to come to Bijoux.

The first fifteen minutes of the show was me walking the crowd through my life, everything that had led up to the moment of me being there. So I showed things like clips from my first *Geordie Shore* audition, which obviously no one had ever seen before, then I'd show scenes from the show that were key moments for me and also talk about why I left. I'd show them the tweets from Gary and at that point the crowd would go wild with everyone chanting, 'Gary's a dick! Gary's a dick!' It was a bit like being in panto with him as the villain – I felt a bit bad . . . although not for long! I was drinking the whole way through, because otherwise I'd have been really nervous.

When the audience first came in, we asked them all to write down a question. Then during the show I sat down with the 'Question Box' and read out their questions. I answered about three or four of them – some were really good and really rude, and you know I'm not shy, so we'd have a bit of fun with them for ten minutes or so. After that it was first interval so we put the music on for everyone to have a dance and go to the bar. That was when it really started turning into a party.

For the next bit Scotty T came out as a surprise. Everyone loves Scotty T – especially the girls. He knows how to get the party going. So we played this segment that we'd pre-recorded. It was a bit like *Through The Keyhole* except we called it *Through The Arsehole*. We pretended to go to someone's house and we'd be really rude about it. It was always Scott's house but people would have to try to guess whose it was the whole way through. Then suddenly there was a huge alarm and everything stopped. We'd announce that there was a golden ticket under someone's seat and the Oompa Loompa song came on while everyone was frantically searching under their seat to see if they've got the golden ticket and had won a place in Bijoux. The lucky person then came up on stage and I shouted, 'Shall we get Willy Wanker out – and find out once and for all whose house we were looking in?' Willy Wanker is obviously our version of Willy Wonka. And of course, it was always Scotty T fully dressed with a purple mask. He strutted on to 'Pony' from *Magic Mike* and then gave the winner a lap dance. Then he'd slowly take the mask off . . . and oh my God the crowd went CRAZY!!!! Once they saw it was Scotty T the girls were WILD! He'd be pouring baby oil all over himself and doing this sexy, funny routine (he did *Dream Boys* so all he had to do was copy the same moves) and everyone lapped it up. Me and Scott are best mates – we're so close we'd do anything for each other – so there was never, ever a doubt he'd do the show with me.

By this point I think we were so drunk it all went a bit mad. We'd get the audience to dare me, Scott and Sophie to do something and then we all just let loose and throw ourselves about on the stage.

I never wanted Jake to come to the show. I was at the stage where I really wanted to be sexy and impress him and me going through my *Geordie Shore* audition tape is NOT AT ALL SEXY! I let his brother Reece come instead; he thought it was hilarious.

But we had such a fun time – we're going to do it again next year and call it 'Mams Go Wild!'. You can't miss it. It's going to be immense.

I might even let Jake come and see it this time . . . if he brings a blindfold and some ear plugs!

Jake and I managed to keep the relationship a secret for a couple of months. This was amazing as it meant we could get to know each other without any pressure. We deliberately didn't follow each other on social media and just did things that were really low key, so no one noticed. I didn't want everyone to know my business – and I knew the press would say it was just another boyfriend to add to the list of so many. Jake wasn't bothered about my antics on *Geordie Shore* because he'd only ever seen a couple of episodes. He also never had a clue I'd done *Celebrity Big Brother* or anything else – he wasn't arsed about fame at all. At first, I thought maybe he was pretending to be cool and then I realised he was being serious. I joked, 'Well that's a bit rude. You need to do some more research!'

Those first few months with Jake really showed me what I'd been missing on the boyfriend front. He treated me like no man had ever treated me in my life. Like taking me to the Maldives for our first holiday and upgrading us to first class! I'd never been first class before, only business class. And it was INSANE.

This was in November. On the first night we were there, he told me I had to be ready at a certain time. Then he walked me to the beach and there was a huge heart-shaped table dug out in the sand, flowers everywhere, a speaker playing Oasis and a three-course meal of all my favourite foods, like prawns to start with and cheesecake for dessert. No one had ever done anything that romantic for me ever! And then he had a little speech and he asked me to be his girlfriend and I said, 'YES! YES! YES!' I kept thinking, 'If this is how I get asked to be his girlfriend – what's a marriage proposal going to be like?' He must have told me mates Adam and Jamie from In the Style, because they sent us a bottle of champagne.

We had such fun out there. One night I got up on stage to sing karaoke and was trying to get the whole bar to get up and dance to Amy Winehouse. Everyone was just sat there glumly so I was shouting, 'Come on! Let go! Have some fun! Fucking get up!!' One of the papers got hold of this story and made out I was telling people to 'Fuck Off back home!' but I was just having a laugh and it was all twisted to sound negative as usual!

When we got home, I just felt so happy. I had the boyfriend of my dreams! I had to pinch myself because he was so perfect but it felt so right and so normal that I also felt a calmness like this was how life was meant to be.

Jake's Do's And Don'ts –
On How To Be A Good Boyfriend

I asked Jake to write this as I think he's so perfect. I thought you might like to leave this page open on your bed for any boyfriends you're with who you wish would learn a thing or two . . .

DO – ensure you are loving, caring and attentive.

DON'T – worry if you haven't always been so thoughtful.
You can change! And you learn from your past behaviour. When I was younger, I made some mistakes – I was dishonest and disloyal in my very first relationship. BUT I also know that relationship shaped me to be the person I am today. The feeling I was left with after making those mistakes genuinely changed my whole attitude going forward in any other relationship. I wasn't ever going to make those mistakes again. I was very young and it taught me a lot. Going forward my attitude towards relationships completely changed. I valued every woman I was with and realised that any relationship I had was very sacred.

DO – embrace romance!
I am very big on wooing a girl because I believe you need to

make the best impression from start to finish on a first date. Here are things I did with Charlotte:

1. I arranged transport for Charlotte to and from the hotel she was staying at in Manchester.
2. When we went for food the waiter didn't have Charlotte's favourite champagne so I paid him extra to pop out to get some from the shops – admittedly she says she prefers Jägerbombs!
3. Opened all doors for her and pulled out her seat.
4. Paid the bill (of course).

Whilst on the date I made sure I learnt loads about Charlotte and her favourite things so I could bank them up for future surprises!

I'm not the only romantic in our relationship though. The most romantic thing Charlotte has ever done for me was doing up my whole apartment with huge lit-up letters spelling out my name for my birthday! She had loads of little presents dotted around and also these lovely cupcakes. No one had ever gone to this much effort for me – I actually got really emotional!

DO – be a team.
To me, love means when you meet your soulmate, which I've met in Charlotte – someone who puts you first, cares about you, respects you, is considerate, does things for you and you do the same for them. I feel like we don't have to try too hard – we just get on. Ultimately you've got to be a team and fully commit to each other.

DO – always make sure you are loyal.

There's no point in entering a relationship if you're not going to be loyal. If you want to explore other people then don't put your partner through it – end the relationship and don't damage a good person.

DON'T – be dishonest.

My main thing in a relationship is being honest, whether you're right or wrong, honesty is key from the beginning as then they will believe you when times are really tested in your relationship.

DO – make sure you are open.

Openness is very important as it helps your partner to understand you fully and get to know you inside and out.

DO – try to be thoughtful.

Being thoughtful and making your partner's day will go a long way and also keep the connection there – it shows that you're always thinking about them.

DO – listen.

This is very important as you can understand your partner's wants and needs, which will make your relationship a lot easier.

DON'T – be distrusting.
Without trust there is no relationship and things will become toxic.

DO – have respect.
Have respect for your partner and also yourself.

DO – compromise.
This is KEY! You can't always do what you want in life and, for the person you love, you have to compromise to find a happy medium.

DO – communicate.
This is also huge in a relationship so you're not second guessing each other.

DON'T – be stubborn.
I like to get my point across if I genuinely believe I have a point to prove. However, if it goes on too long and you're not getting anywhere, you need to have the ability to walk away, cool down and try to understand the other person's point of view. In the grand scheme of things – is this argument even worth it? Then you should take a commonsense approach to get the argument resolved as soon as possible! Going to bed on an argument is never a nice feeling and often drags it out. A lot of people let their stubbornness get the better of them and some of the silliest of arguments turn into something massive.

NUMBER ONE RULE – FORGET BEING RIGHT AND STOP BEING STUBBORN! Also, try making the first move and apologise – you won't believe where it gets you!

What's funny is, after I asked Jake to write this, I found my own dating tips from my first book *Me Me Me*. Let's see how they match up!

A note of advice from me (aged twenty-five)
about how to be a good boyfriend:

1. Do be charming and confident.
2. Don't tell the girl she reminds you of an animal.
3. Don't show them your penis (Gary did that on his dates; he showed girls pictures of his penis).
4. Don't ask about their favourite sex position.
5. Do be funny and witty.
6. Don't say you need a poo.
7. Do look nice.
8. Don't be suicidal.
9. Do have some self-esteem.

I think we can all agree that Jake's advice is better!

5

My baby is . . .

the best news ever

Jake and I had such a great time in the lead-up to Christmas and our bond got stronger and stronger. There was a lot of conversation about the future, which shocked me because in any other relationship I'd ever had, talking about babies was a NO GO subject. I couldn't even look at a baby in a pram without the fear setting in their eyes. But we both knew we wanted children, and we couldn't stop talking about having them. But when Jake told me he wanted to be a dad I was both relieved and then worried – what if I couldn't give him what he wanted?!

I was always concerned that it was going to be a hard process because of my reproductive system. After the ectopic pregnancy in 2016, Mr Okaro told me that I might struggle to get pregnant. He didn't say it was impossible, but that it would probably take longer than normal. Getting pregnant isn't always an easy thing – even when everything's working. So in my head, I thought it was going to take at least a couple of years. But what if it took longer? What if it never happened at all? It started really worrying me. It had always been in the back of my head but, because previous boyfriends hadn't wanted kids, I hadn't had to confront it. After Gary and the shock and upset of it all I had never actually tried. I didn't try with Joshua (he was enough of a baby himself!), I didn't try with Liam because he was clear he wasn't interested. I always wanted kids, but I hadn't met anyone who I felt was good enough to be a father or who didn't panic at the idea of it.

And now I had found the right person, what if I couldn't give him what he wanted? Jake was so wonderful and assured me that he was with me for me, and that a kid would be a bonus but if we couldn't have one he still wanted to be with me more than anything. And also, there are so many other avenues you can go down, like adoption. But my biological clock was beeping in my face and screaming at me to get on with it! So, we decided we would try. Then obviously both of us got really overcome with emotion and started blubbing our eyes out at the thought of being parents. We cry so often it's ridiculous! Whenever we're out in public, people must think we're either mad, have just had a row or have been chopping loads of onions!

It's amazing to think that I managed to keep our relationship private for so long before even really talking about Jake or posting pictures of him. And because I wasn't doing a TV show (or writing a book!) I didn't have the need or the pressure to tell the world. It was so lovely being able to get to know each other behind closed doors, and so refreshing that Jake had zero interest in being in the public eye. He has a private Instagram and couldn't give a toss about having any followers or being famous – the complete opposite to any of my exes! What I think I enjoyed the most was actually not having anyone poke their nose in or offer an opinion on what I was doing or whether he was right for me. Don't get me wrong, I know my fans care about me and people worry about me falling in love too easily . . . but this was perfect. I didn't have to share it with the world. I could just enjoy getting to know someone and falling in love, without people having their opinions saying, 'Oh not *another one*, Charlotte!?'

On that note, can I just say that just because someone has had a few boyfriends don't make it out to be a negative. All it means is that they don't stand for shit and they respected themselves enough to leave that relationship and not be walked all over. It just turns out that some of the men in my life have been in it for the wrong reasons . . . and I had to walk away. So those sorts of comments don't really help. I mean, would you rather I was still with Stephen Bear or Joshua Ritchie, the shitheads?! I don't think so! These idiots happened for a reason and led me to the happy-ever-after I have now. I have waited for the person who would treat me like the best human. And that's Jake. He is everything I ever wanted. So, for anyone reading this, if you're being treated like shit and are too scared to start again and leave the bad boyfriend – please have a word with yourself right now! Give yourself a slap! Look at yourself in the mirror and say, 'I deserve more than this. I am not scared to start over and go through this process all over again. Because I am amazing, and I deserve more. So I'm going to press the "fuck off" button and jump off the precipice of the unknown . . .'

Jake and I started trying for a baby at the end of 2021. I spent nearly every day constantly googling the possibilities and kept finding people on Instagram saying things like, 'I got pregnant by my boyfriend after a month!' I would look in the mirror and tell myself, 'Positive vibes only!' I thought that if I imagined I was pregnant then it would happen (if Mary did it with Jesus – why couldn't I have an immaculate conception?). January 2022 was the slowest month ever! I stared at my calendar waiting for the date when my period was due (and praying that I'd be late). But the day before I was due, I woke with really bad cramps. My heart sank and I shuffled to the toilet, scared that any sudden or fast movement might affect my chances of holding in a baby. I sat on the loo and looked down. There was just a big red pool of blood in my knickers. I put my head in my hands and cried and cried. I told Jake and I could tell he was disappointed, but he was more concerned about me and told me to try not to worry and that maybe it just wasn't the right time.

We'd both been so incredibly excited. Despite being told it was going to be more difficult for me because of my history, there was just a hopefulness that it was going to happen. I think loads of couples feel like that and expect it will happen straight away somehow. But now we had the realisation that I had only one fallopian tube that works and it wasn't going to be simple. After we'd processed the disappointment and had a few tears we sat down and held each other's hands.

'Let's book a nice holiday,' he said, as he hugged me tightly, 'let's enjoy some more time together, going out having fun and living our lives.'

It was only a couple of months since he'd asked me to be his girlfriend in the Maldives. We should go away together again, get drunk and really enjoy each other's company. 'You're so right,' I sighed. 'We've literally known each other for a grand total of three and a half months. Maybe it just wasn't meant to be.'

The thing is though, deep down, I never ever felt like it was too soon. I just knew Jake was *the one*. But I knew I needed to be sensible and chill out about it.

We got on our phones and we found the earliest date we could get time off work and booked a nice holiday for

March – an all-inclusive hotel in Mexico. 'Let's make it party central!' I declared. 'Let's have some fun!'

The very next day, we even went to the shop and bought ovulation sticks – so that I *wouldn't* get pregnant before the holiday. I wasn't on any contraception, so we figured that if we had a more accurate indication of the days I was due to ovulate we would just have to avoid having sex on those days. At this point, I was thinking, 'It's going to be a bit of a hard journey. It's going to be difficult, it might not happen, but I'm going to try not to let it linger in my head. I'm going to enjoy being with Jake and I'm going to enjoy this holiday. There's absolutely no rush.'

A Valentine's Day with a difference

February came and Jake had planned a special few days as it was our first Valentine's Day together. He whisked me off to London to this beautiful hotel and had laid rose petals everywhere . . . EVERYWHERE. There was a bottle of Captain Morgan's Spiced Rum – I realise this kind of ruins the story as it would sound better with champagne, but I like spiced rum better – and I poured myself a glass and started drinking. But I couldn't even finish it! WHAT WAS WRONG WITH ME?! I was not in the mood to drink at all. And I couldn't work out why. And then I remembered, I'd felt like that the week before too!

I'd gone to the Brit Awards and the whole night I'd been in an awful strop. Everyone was drinking but I'd felt ill. I'd been thinking, 'I can't get these drinks down! I feel sick.' And I felt like I was ruining everyone's night, so I ended up going home early. I'd been there with Sophie and she'd told me I was in a vile mood – she'd given me so much shit afterwards!

So here I was in the hotel and feeling like dog shit again. I also felt bad because Jake was watching me expectantly, thinking he'd pulled off the best surprise – meanwhile, I'm sat there with a face like a slapped arse. An arse that can't handle any alcohol.

Wow, this was not going well. And then, to make things even worse, obviously Jake wanted to have sex – as you do, it's Valentine's! – but I wasn't feeling it. My vagina was so dry you would not believe. I'll tell you how dry it was – when I got in the bath later on, I felt my vagina in the water and IT WAS STILL LIKE THE SAHARA DESERT! It was like sandpaper down there. How on earth your vagina is dry underwater is beyond me. But that is how dry my vagina was! By this point, Jake was now unconscious in the corner having passed out because he drank more booze than I did. The poor guy must have fallen asleep thinking, 'She doesn't want to drink. She doesn't want to have sex. She must not be into me any more!' At the same time, I'm panicking that he's going to think he's spent all this money on me to surprise me and I'm being so moody and ungrateful. We were both worrying that the other person had gone off us, but we weren't talking about it!

The next day, I realised I was due for my period. So, I said to Jake, 'I'm so sorry, I didn't realise, it must have been my hormones.'

He was relieved, 'Ah right, OK, that's fair enough.'

We were both dead happy that we'd found the answer as to why I'd been such a total and utter bitch.

But then my period didn't come.

What?

Maybe it's tomorrow?

Maybe it's the stress of us thinking we don't like each other any more?

I woke up the next day . . .

. . . still no period.

There's no way I could be pregnant. We did not have sex on days when that ovulation stick had a smiley face! We avoided that day completely so there is no way I can be pregnant.

A couple of days went by and, for some reason, I started waking up at 5am every single morning. And I don't know whether anyone else has had this experience in the very beginning stage of being pregnant, but I had this weird insomnia where you wake up loads of times. I messaged my best friend from school, Natalie, who lives in Australia, because I knew she'd be up because of the time difference.

'Natalie, something's not right. I've not come on my period. I keep waking up at random times. I can't stomach a drink. And I'm being a bit moody.'

'I think you need to get a pregnancy test tomorrow.'

I woke up in the morning, went straight to the shop, bought a test and took it back to our hotel. The football was on TV, so Jake was in the other room – he's football crazy so was totally engrossed. I'd told him I was going to do a test, but he'd forgotten in an instant because it was a big match on. So, while he was watching it, I weed on the pregnancy test and waited.

I watched it and within about a minute . . .

LO AND FUCKING BEHOLD I WAS PREGNANT!

And honestly, I didn't know what to do with myself.

Obviously I was over the moon because there'd been times I never thought I'd see that in my whole life – but I was also shocked and scared because we'd convinced ourselves this wasn't the right time, that we'd been thinking about it too soon, and we'd planned our holiday in Mexico.

I went into this state of panic.

My body's about to change. My whole life is about to change. I'm actually pregnant! This might even destroy our relation-ship – we've only just got together! I love him so much I don't want things to change anything . . .

All these worries were in my head, which I know now are just totally normal worries . . . and then another big one came:

MY WHOLE FREEDOM HAS GONE! MY WHOLE LIFE HAS GONE!

Even though I was the person who wanted a baby so much, who desperately wanted to know that it was going to be OK and I was going to conceive . . . then all of a sudden, I'm freaking out. It was the weirdest feeling. I think a lot of people do relate to it though. When I called Natalie, she said, 'Charlotte, I've been with Kurt for sixteen years but when I saw that positive test, I went out for a walk for two hours alone to get my thoughts together.' What was I panicking about??'

And then I thought, 'Shit, am I going to be a hormonal bitch for nine months? How is he going to put up with me? Is he going to want sex if my fanny is like sandpaper? He's going to hate me!'

When Jake came in and saw the test he was ecstatic. He was in shock too, but he was SO, SO HAPPY. Meanwhile, I was still processing it all. I honestly couldn't talk for about two hours – I was crying my eyes out, then silence, then I'd cry again. I just said to him, 'I'm in shock. And I'm all scared.'

Finally, I calmed down and the two days after that were more romantic than anything I could ever dream of. We were still staying in the hotel, so went down to the spa. We were kissing for ages in the pool. We were staring into each other's eyes and honestly it was a connection that I've never felt with anyone else. We were looking at each other thinking, 'We've created a life! What the hell?' We were just so in that moment, it was so perfect I'll never forget the feeling. The mad thing was I actually started to get horny again. The vagina was wet again after the dry spell. But because we were in a public pool in the spa, we couldn't do anything about it. There were a lot of other people about who must have been thinking, 'Go to your room, guys!' Also we had massages booked, so by the time we got back to the hotel room my vagina was dry again so we didn't get to be horny parents-to-be after all.

After that we went to see my doctor, Mr Okaro. Because I'd had the ectopic, he'd told me that any pregnancy I had after that was high risk as I might have another one, so I needed to see him straight away. Thank God we were already in London – it was like it was meant to be! When I suffered my ectopic, I was rushed to the St John and St Elizabeth Hospital in London – it was so horrendous, I was on the verge of dying, I'd literally passed out and was convulsing. I'd been internally bleeding for a week and if I'd been left any longer, that would be it, I would be dead. I wouldn't be here now. But Mr Okaro – the one who had saved my life – happened to be around the corner from our hotel in that same hospital. How is that not meant to be? I AM ROUND THE CORNER FROM MY DOCTOR JUST WHEN I FIND OUT I'M PREGNANT?! I immediately rang him up, 'I'm pregnant, I'm terrified and I need to know it's in the right place and it's not in the fallopian tube again.' We literally got booked in for the day afterwards. So, we took ourselves off to the hospital, had our first scan, and our baby was all nice and tucked up like a tiny little thing – in the womb, not in the fallopian tube.

I'm getting emotional again just thinking about it, but it was just so wonderful. I genuinely believe everything that's happened between me and Jake has been destiny. I look at him and feel so happy and content.

The moment we found out we were having a baby together Jake kept saying how he just couldn't wait to experience it all with me. He said, 'The whole journey will be perfect with you by my side. We've not known each other that long and we're still finding out about each other every day, we have a pretty good knowledge of each other but I feel like being a parent and being with the woman I love the most – nothing can top that!' He tells me so many amazing things like how much he fancies me, but he says it's my personality that he fell in love with most. He says I'm the funniest person he knows and that he loves having a laugh with me. I love the fact we could just be sitting in a room and we'd laugh all day. He said the other day that he loves the way I am with people, because I put in time and effort and am caring and kind. It's so refreshing to see. But I see the same with him – we both put each other first.

I carry you around everywhere I go
For three whole months no one can know
I can feel you move, I love the sound of your heart
But what's to come will be my favourite part
So many first times I'm waiting to come
When you look in my eyes, or when you hold my thumb
When I think of you, in my throat I feel a lump
Can't wait to meet you, my beautiful bump

I wrote this poem in the notes on my phone the day after I found out I was pregnant. It was the most incredible and magical thing in the world to have happened to me. At that moment I just felt so incredibly lucky.

An A-Z Of My Boyfriend Jake

A

Articulate. Jake loves to explain and get his points across properly – especially with his emotions and I love that SO MUCH about him.

B

Bum. Jake has the most squidgy bum and I always, *always* slap it.

C

Caring. I have never ever, EVER, EVER met anyone as caring as Jake.

D

Dates. Jake LOVES organising dates. It's soooooo nice having someone make that effort and take control.

E

Ears. Although I honestly don't think they are big now, they were the first thing I noticed about Jake. But I was really *attracted* to his big ears – I actually thought they were so CUTE. People always take the piss out of them though!

F

Family. Jake's very family orientated and I also love his family so much! I get on so well with his mam, it's like we've known each other forever, and his brother means the world to me.

G

Get up and go! Jake is so driven to succeed. He is always pushing himself to do better and be better. I love that about him.

H

Haaland. Jake's fave footballer ever.

I

Igloo. Jake's very impressed with my igloo-building skills. I've told him we can make one together one day. He's excited.

J

Jake Junior. A name we would love to call a little boy if we had one.

K

King of Clean. Jake LOVES cleaning and tidying. Honestly he's the cleanest person I know (total opposite to me!).

L

Loved. I've never felt as loved by anyone in my life. Jake makes me feel like the only girl in the world.

M

Muscles. Jake has the most gorgeous shoulders, arms and pecs. And he doesn't even have to go to the gym for those muscles, he was just born with them.

N

Never ever late. Jake is super organised in every aspect of life and that includes punctuality (unlike me!).

O

Oh-amazing in between the sheets.

P

Pep Guardiola Manchester City manager, who Jake actually thinks is the best thing since sliced bread!

Q

Quitter. When Jake gets too stressed with something, he often gives up.

R

Rolls-Royce. Jake's dream cars – there's a convertible one and a four-wheel drive on the list if he wins the lottery.

S

Sensitive. Jake is such a big softie.

T

Together. He actually loves me even more when we are together every day. We are like two little best friends who never leave each other's side.

U

Underwear. Jake wears F&F boxers from Tesco and they are so comfy. I stole them the whole way through pregnancy.

V

Very headstrong! He knows what he wants and he's confident about getting it and fighting for it.

W

Willy. He has a lovely willy.

X

x. One of Ed Sheeran's albums, who Jake absolutely LOVES. It was the first concert he booked for us to go to together.

Y

Yin and Yang. I do believe Jake is my soul mate – he's the Yin to my Yang. Even though we're the same in so many ways, he's opposite to me in his cleanliness and organisation. He's a very private person and I'm very public. But we have the same values and are both really emotional and we just work perfectly together.

Z

Zebras. One of the animals I want to take him to see on a safari in South Africa for one of our first family holidays.

6

My baby is . . .

hard to keep a secret

Jake and I decided to hide the pregnancy news from people because we didn't want anyone knowing before we knew it was all properly safe. Kate, my agent, was the first person I told. She'd made the appointment at the hospital in London when I'd found out. But I didn't even tell Mam and Dad. I knew I would have another scan at six weeks to check the heartbeat was there, and I was nervous because two of my friends had just been through miscarriages and they were obviously devastated.

I told myself it was best not to tell anyone until I'd had that scan, but me mam was starting to suspect because I was getting so sick all the time. One day, when I was in the car with her she just randomly asked, 'Are you pregnant? I had a dream that you were.'

And I looked all sheepish . . . 'No. It was just a dream!'

But then she said, 'You keep saying you're tired all the time and you look a mess!'

In the end I told her two days before the six-week scan, I couldn't hold it in any longer! For some reason I knew everything was going to be OK, like it was an instinct, a gut feeling.

When we told her and Dad, I was so nervous! I planned this whole night. We were going to order in a Chinese and pretend that there was a TikTok trend to do with fortune cookies. What Mam didn't know was that I'd found this special place that made custom fortune cookies. So my plan was that Mam and Dad would open them, and inside it would say, 'Can't wait to meet you, Grandad!' and the next one would say, 'Can't wait to meet you, Nana!'

I'd got another pregnancy test so that once they'd cracked the fortune cookies open I could slide the positive test across the table to prove to them it was for real. I didn't have a clue how they would react. Me dad is very chilled out but I didn't know how Mam would respond at all.

On the night of Operation Baby I felt like we were waiting ages before we could go over to their house. Jake was so quiet because he was all nerves like me. We arrived with the Chinese and told them we all needed to open our fortune cookies. Jake was first to throw them off because his said something random like, 'You are a speaker of words and a doer of deeds . . . and your lucky number is twenty-five.'

I told them both they needed to open their cookies at the same time. 'One, two, three . . .!' Mam put her glasses on so she could read the words and the first thing she said was, 'Oh it's tiny! How am I going to see this?'

Then Mam opened the one that said, 'Can't wait to meet you, Grandad' . . . and Dad opened the one that said, 'Can't wait to meet you, Nana'. I'd had one job to do and I'd given them the wrong cookies!

Jake and I were trying our hardest not to scream.

Then they both looked at me, realisation on their faces. And I pulled the test out from my bra and put it on the counter.

Dad said, 'You're not!?'

'I am!' I smiled.

Mam clutched her chest and said, 'Oh my God! Are you really??!'

They were both so in shock and so happy. We were all in tears as Mam came over to hug me and then Dad hugged Jake. Mam said to him, 'Jake! Thank you so much! You've got good sperm!'

I said to Mam, 'See! You knew! You'd been saying it all this time!'

'I didn't actually think you *were* pregnant!' she laughed. She couldn't believe it.

*　　*　　*

What a night that was. The stress of the whole day made me pull all my eyelashes off my left eye. And I bit off every single nail. It was so incredible. What a time to be alive and what a huge moment to have. I went to sleep in the biggest happy bubble.

Two days later we had the scan – I was so nervous. I don't think I'd have cared if I saw just a potato if it had a heartbeat. I was just so excited because it was my first baby. I screamed, 'Oh my God – there's a baby in there!' Just seeing the baby, still there in the correct place with a healthy beating pulse was nothing short of a miracle to me. I didn't expect to see much movement but the baby had other plans – it was like a little acrobat in there turning and spinning and rolling around. I was in awe!

Of all the reactions of the people I told – my favourite moment was with Nana Jean. God I miss her so much. I'm so so happy she was still with us for this moment but my heart breaks every time I think about the fact I will never see her again and she didn't get to be a great-nana for more than a few weeks. I can vividly recall the moment we told her the news – she was wearing this cute little green jumper that I'd bought her and was looking so adorable. Mam was filming it all, but she ended up doing a really crap job because she started crying halfway through! It's the happiest I've ever seen my nana and I couldn't stop smiling afterwards. She has always wanted a great-grandchild and she was just beaming from ear to ear; it was so damn cute. If only she had been able to be there for longer.

When we told Jake's mam Natalie she was over the moon too. And her and me mam really bonded over it when we introduced them on Mothers' Day – they kept being really funny together and they were calling each other 'Grandma' (that's Natalie) and 'Nana' (which is me mam). Mam went through a phase of wanting to be called Grandma but I told her that was weird because in the North-East you call your grandmother 'Nana' and that's it. Grandma sounded too posh for her. So we gave that to Natalie. The pair of them get on so well and I love them being first-time grandparents together.

It was so DAMN HARD keeping it from everyone else though. I couldn't let anyone know in case it came out in the press. I spent the whole time having to cancel plans with friends and making up excuses about work. And I had just released my Blitz n Burn fitness app! People say that the first trimester is the hardest bit, because that's when your body is physically creating the baby and all its organs and stuff – but that's when no one knows it's going on and you can't tell people!

The app had seemed like a great idea when we came up with it – back in October – because I'd been getting so into my fitness in lockdown and after the break-up with Liam, so it just seemed like a natural progression. I'd been really successful with my workout programs in the past – I'd had the best-selling fitness DVDs in the UK (still in shock about that if I'm honest!). When we recorded the workouts I was feeling better than ever, but when the app launched I was pregnant and physically exhausted all the time. Any exercise I tried to do – I couldn't breathe. And because it was the launch of the app, I needed to be on it constantly, doing live workouts! In the end, I had to tell my trainer, David, and of course he said that I shouldn't be doing such intense workouts. So he put me on slightly easier moves, but I was still SHATTERED!!! It couldn't have been worse timing!

It was EVEN MORE DIFFICULT keeping it from Sophie. She knows me so well and she kept going, 'I know something's up. You just haven't been yourself,' and she kept saying that over and over again. She was adamant I was pregnant. She would look at me and say, 'I can just tell!' And because she was supporting me and doing the app with me, I was physically having to work out with her even though I was feeling ill and couldn't breathe. But I couldn't cancel because she was on to me! Looking back, this probably wasn't the best reason to overdo it . . .

If we went out a few days later she would be at it again. 'You haven't been out in a while – you're sure you're not pregnant?'

'Nah! Don't be silly!'

After that, when I did go out, I'd have to make a point of always having a drink in my hand in photos and pretending to sip it. I'd make sure I had a glass of wine in a boomerang so no one would ever suspect.

I wanted to tell Sophie and Holly in a really special way. We'd all been booked to go on *Geordie Shore: The Reunion 2022* so that gave me the perfect opportunity. But I knew I had to wait until we started filming as I wanted it to be really natural. I wanted to get their genuine reactions on camera when they heard for the first time. This meant I could not give up the facade that I was putting on. Sophie still says to this day, 'How did you come to the gym with me and keep that all a secret?!' I didn't know I could be such a good liar! This was the biggest secret I'd ever managed to keep – turns out I'm very, very good at fibbing!

Just before I was about to break the news to the girls, Jake and I flew away to Dubai for a little break. We'd cancelled the Mexico holiday in the end because it was all planned around boozing. Dubai was such a wonderful trip because I was able to take it all in, I would sit on the sun loungers with Jake and we'd pore over the baby scans and be in awe of what we'd created!

Announcing it to the world

Once we'd filmed the show (I'll tell you all about that later), it was time to tell the world. To officially announce my pregnancy, I posted a video on my Instagram of the moment I had shown Jake the positive test. I felt so nervous in the lead-up to uploading it – I didn't have a clue what people would say. I was praying that everyone would be nice! I also felt bad because I'm such an honest person and I knew I'd been keeping this massive secret from the world!

Well, the reaction from the public was out of this world. Wow.

It was so amazing. I couldn't believe it. It wasn't just fans either. There were even comments from so many brands who I don't even work with – all sharing the news. It was all over Pretty Little Thing, boohoo, Ego . . . all these businesses sharing my news. *Grazia* magazine wrote a lovely piece online saying how I had given hope to so many women who were struggling to conceive. And I had loads of people messaging saying the same thing, that they'd been so worried it might not happen for them but that I'd now made them feel more positive about the future.

One woman said she had been trying for six months and still hadn't got pregnant, but this gave her hope. So many others were telling me how they knew how difficult my journey had been with reproductive health and for women that have had similar experiences, my news was even more inspiring.

Anyone else lying in bed crying at Charlotte Crosby's pregnancy announcement video or just me?

I have been watching @Charlottegshore on Geordie
Shore since I was 17/18 & I'm now 30 – to know she
is expecting a baby after so much crap she has been
through!! I'm so happy for her & Jake!! It couldn't
have happened to a better person!

That evening I went up to bed and I started sobbing my
eyes out. I had the nicest realisation. I thought, 'I honestly
couldn't be any happier in life right now. I just feel so
lucky and like everything is just falling into place.' I was
looking around my beautiful home thinking I was finally
back where I belong, about to start my own family with the
most amazing man – the most loving, caring man that I've
ever met in my life. It was such an incredible feeling. I was
walking up the stairs and just in bits. I was thinking back to
when I'd first got the house a few years ago. I remembered
looking up at the staircase envisaging seeing my children up
there (imaginary ones obviously) and thinking about them
one day standing on the bottom step for their first-day-at-
school photo, or sitting on them for family photos. And now,
to walk up the same set of stairs and to really truly imagine
the laughter of my beautiful baby echoing through the walls.
It just made everything I'd been through in life feel right!
Every dead end I'd turned down, every wrong person I'd
met and dated, all of it had led me to this moment. I knew
I was about to start a brand new chapter surrounded by all
the people I love.

I felt a massive relief that I didn't have to hide my pregnancy any more. But, because the public and the press had gone so wild over the news, I suddenly got scared to go out! I had gone from no one being all that bothered about me to ALL this attention, with people watching and waiting for the first pregnancy photo! I decided I was better just staying in the house. I wanted to let the dust settle before I went out again. Before all this, people had always been really lovely to me if I saw them in the streets – would ask how I was and want a photo – but this time I knew they would all want to say congratulations and talk to me. I was still at the point where I was feeling ill and I got all scared and anxious about it!

But I was desperate for some milk and needed to do some food shopping. There's a Marks and Spencer right next to my house where they treat me mam like Lady Gaga. Every single staff member in that M&S knows Letitia Crosby; she buys them all presents and knows them all by name. She's literally like royalty. So, in turn, they're always talking to me, but it's always just about me mam. 'I haven't seen Letitia, is she OK? She hasn't been in this week.' So, as it is my most local shop and one of the little ones that's never that busy, I asked Mam to come there with me. I was so nervous about going in and feeling overwhelmed in case everyone was talking about me. And I was feeling really sick as well. In the end we got there in the car and parked and I said, 'Can you go in for me? I'll give you a little list.' Mam said, 'OK, see you in a few minutes,' and off she went inside.

I sat in that car for two and a half hours.

The list only had ten things on it! When she returned I said, 'Mam – what the hell?!'

And she replied, 'Charlotte! I couldn't get round! Everyone was stopping me wanting to talk about you. Saying, "Congratulations, you're going to be a nana." I honestly couldn't get round the shop because every single person, the shop assistants, all the customers were stopping me! It's a good job you didn't come in there!'

So our baby news was out in the open, a new chapter of life was beginning and everyone was coming along for the ride. It was such an incredible feeling, but I was also a bit worried that I'd never be able to do a normal food shop again in peace! What if I started to get mad cravings and needed to go and buy a big bar of soap to put in a sandwich or something?! The whole world would have an opinion on it! I'm joking of course – my cravings were never that exciting. But it's funny how some pregnant women get mad urges to eat bricks and lumps of sponge! The female body can be a truly weird and wonderful thing.

It can also be painful and heart-breaking too – as me mam was about to find out.

7

My baby is . . .

a ray of light among some dark clouds

Jake moved permanently into my place in May 2022. Before that we were splitting our time between my house and his flat in Manchester but there was never a question of him not coming to live with me. Not only was I not keen to move away after my Bolton experience with Josh, Jake always wanted to be where I was most happy. He's so confident and relaxed, he can settle anywhere and it doesn't bother him. He is so crazily independent that he just does what he feels is right at the time. For example, he told me that when he was eighteen and his grandma died, he was really upset about it. But she had left him some money so, instead of moping about, Jake decided he would go on an adventure in her honour. On Christmas Eve, he upped and left his mam and dad and said, 'Right, I'm off to Florida!' They took him to the airport and he flew to Florida, spent Christmas on his own and went to a theme park. What an absolute nutter! He says he did make friends with an Irish family, who obviously took pity on him being out there alone, but he was perfectly happy. And then on New Year's Eve, he sat on the balcony of his hotel room watching the fireworks all by himself. You'd think he was an only child with that sort of behaviour!

Jake is just very good at dealing with new situations and embraces life and lives it to the full. And as soon as he moved up he found his own little places he liked – like a barber round the corner, a sunbed shop and a gym he always goes to. He probably knows more people around here than I do! He's just so different to anyone I've been with before, because he's confident and happy in his own skin. He deals with any situation and just gets on with it. And as soon as he came to my place he made me feel like he wanted to be there and was instantly part of my life. It made me love him even more because he just started fixing things and doing stuff that needed doing around the house that I'd never got round to doing, He doesn't just look after me – he looks after our home too.

Not all news is good news . . .

It felt like we'd only been able to enjoy the excitement of the pregnancy for a few minutes before we got the worst news ever. Mam had breast cancer.

We found out the day after my birthday in May. She'd gone for a normal routine mammogram – she had no symptoms, there were no signs. When she got back from the mammogram they called and said they'd seen something like a shadow and she needed to go for a biopsy. I was convinced it would just be nothing. Mam on the other hand kept stressing and saying, 'I know it's cancer.' I said to her, 'You always worry every time about stuff like this and then it's nothing.'

Jake had taken me away to a spa hotel for a treat and we were in the hotel when we got the news. Mam had heard back from the hospital and been told that her worst fears had come true. She phoned me up in tears, she was hysterical. Jake already knew it was coming, because she had been texting him first because she was so worried about telling me.

I got off the phone and broke down in Jake's arms and sobbed and sobbed. He was so amazing, stroking my hair and telling me we needed to be positive and that we'd get through it, she would be OK.

I felt like I was living in a nightmare. But I told myself that this was the last time I was going to cry – I was going to pull myself together and be strong for me mam. Everything to do with my pregnancy had vanished. I felt ill and was throwing up all the time but I was just not even there in my mind.

The rest of that month was so emotional. May and June were just the worst because we were waiting and waiting to get answers, not knowing how bad it was, not knowing if it was curable. It was just horrendous and me mam was spiralling out of control. She thought she was going to die. She was floored. She'd just had the best news ever – that she was going to be a nana for the first time – and then this.

Mam couldn't get out of her dark place. She was just struggling to process what had happened. She was constantly in tears. She went into such a negative zone in her mind. And there are only so many times you can tell yourself your mam is going to be OK, when your mam is saying, 'I am going to die, I am going to die.'

I spent hours with her every day, trying to take her mind off stuff and get her out of that headspace. I was doing anything I could to make her laugh. But the second I left her side she was back again, hitting rock bottom, so unbelievably low.

But although I was holding it together on the outside, I was so incredibly stressed in my body. Whenever I got home from being with Mam, I'd lie in bed with Jake just staring at the ceiling and thinking, 'She could actually die.' It was the worst feeling ever, we should have been so happy but there was this awful dark cloud of not knowing what the future was going to hold.

Mam went for tests to see what type of cancer it was and the day she was due to get her results it was Holly's wedding in Ibiza – and I was a bridesmaid. I desperately wanted to be there for me mam as I knew how much she needed me, but I couldn't let Holly down. I was also feeling ill and throwing up, still having the worst pregnancy ever. Jake was keeping in touch with Mam at home and checking in on her every five minutes to see if the results had come in. I don't know what I would have done without him. He was so amazing. All the upset with me mam just brought us even closer together. He has done absolutely everything for me. He's amazing. If he could hear me so much as start to retch – he would sprint down to the toilet to pull back my hair. He was by my side for the whole wedding, and he was there with me at the end of the phone when Mam called with the results.

Thankfully the news was better than we'd feared. The lump was very small – about the size of a Malteser – and it was in its early stages, which immediately put us all back in better spirits although Mam was shocked, because she hadn't been able to feel it at all. After that she was told she had to have some more biopsies to see exactly where it was, how much of the breast would have to be taken away and whether it had spread. They knew they needed to take more than the tumour but needed to work out how much. Caulk is a kind of calcium that forms in your breast that can indicate where the cancer might return, so they need to get the margins right to make sure they remove it all. Normally you have one biopsy, and they can tell from that everything they need to know for the surgery. But Mam had to have three because they were coming back as inconclusive. The biopsies were so painful for her. I went to hospital with her each time, and I just hated knowing that she was about to go through all that pain again. They were sticking this big, long rod in her poor boob and it was black and blue, it was so bruised. The nurses felt so guilty because they kept saying, 'We've never had to do this so many times!'

Finally, it was third time lucky (if you can call it luck) and what came back was that the area around the lump, called the calcium flex, looked as if it was infected. So that all needed to be removed. We got her surgery booked in as soon as possible and she was given a date for the hospital at the end of June.

Every cloud has a (pink) lining

We decided to have the gender-reveal party for the baby at the beginning of June, a few days before Mam was due to have her surgery. This way, we thought, she could let her hair down a bit and not worry. No one at the party knew she was ill as we didn't want to make it public or make a big thing about it – but obviously she got drunk and started telling a few people throughout the evening!

I always wanted to have a gender-reveal party because I loved seeing them on shows in Hollywood – the Kardashians are great at throwing lavish parties for their baby-to-be and I wanted the same! Plus, I didn't ever want to keep the sex of the little one a surprise because I don't like surprises! Surely having a baby is going to be a surprise enough? I wanted to be able to properly prepare so I could get all excited by clothes shopping and stuff.

You know me, I'm not one to do things subtly or by halves, so I was determined that the gender-reveal party was going to be THE BIGGEST EVENT EVER, which meant there was a lot to organise. When I look back though, the gender-reveal party was so much less stressful than the baby shower – the baby shower was hell on earth but we'll come on to that later!

Jake and I had matching outfits – both bright orange! I knew orange would make us stand out and wouldn't get people thinking we knew what the sex of the baby was. We couldn't have worn blue or pink because that would have thrown out the whole point of the party! I had an outfit made especially by a woman I've used whenever I've wanted a dress to make a statement! She's done lots of my red-carpet looks. I told her I wanted something really different, and she definitely delivered. I basically copied the Kardashians! I am usually one for plain dresses or something a bit more understated – but this was ALL OUT. And when I say all out, I literally mean it, because it was an orange sparkly jumpsuit with one leg completely cut out – I basically had my arse cheek showing – and the other completely covered. The material even went over the shoe itself. It was unique and different – definitely not to be forgotten. But a few days before the event I started getting really paranoid and questioning whether it was appropriate for me – a mother-to-be – to be wearing something so out there? I think it was the hormones because I was really up and down. One minute, I'd look at the outfit and think it was amazing, and then next thing I'd be crying that I would look an embarrassing orange idiot. I never usually give a shit, so it must have been my mind messing with me.

The party was in the rooftop bar of The Vermont Hotel in Newcastle, which is sort of funky. I always wanted something really different and cool and we had so many little touches like a doughnut wall and a board for people to write their gender predictions. There were over a hundred guests and each person was told that they had to wear the brightest colours possible – no wallflowers allowed! I wanted neon sparkle, glitter, feathers, dresses like rainbows! Then I obviously got loads of texts beforehand from people saying, 'I'm stressed! I don't know what to wear!'

So I replied, 'Just wear something fucking colourful. It's really not that hard!'

It was mainly the lads to be honest, they're so used to just wearing black, white and grey clothes. But the clue was in the word – COLOURFUL.

I was determined that this would be a party unlike anyone else's – and there was no expense spared. I also wanted to find out the sex of our baby in a way that felt unique – not just cutting a cake or bursting a balloon. So, I decided we'd get a plane to fly over and reveal it – because I'd never seen that done before. We booked this skywriter who was going to fly over the bar and the smoke that came out behind would be either blue or pink, depending on the sex of the baby. I didn't know (as that's the whole point!) so I had to get Kate to speak to the hospital so they could tell her, and she could tell the skywriter. So, as usual, Kate was the first person to know my most intimate information, before anyone else!

I was actually sitting with her when she got the email from the hospital telling her the gender. I looked at her face trying to read what it meant but she just started laughing and walked away. This then stressed me right out and I kept wanting to know – without *really* wanting to know! I couldn't look her in the eye for ages after that. It's so weird how your stress levels are when you're pregnant. Stuff you think you can deal with just flies out of the window with the hormone situation. Sometimes you feel like you can't even breathe!

> *Growing fast inside of me,*
> *On Sunday we'll find out what you will be,*
> *Pink or blue – come what may,*
> *Just the thought of our family makes our day!*
> *Either or, we do not mind,*
> *As long as you're healthy and grow up to be kind.*

When the day came, oh my God, THE NERVES! I don't know whether it was because I was about to finally find out the gender of my child, or because so many people were going to be there and a lot of them were people I'd never met before. Loads of Jake's friends were coming over who I hadn't even met in a normal situation. So I had a two-hour nap which sorted me out. Sleep is the cure for everything!

117

You know how I said that I have manifested stuff? And that I always knew in my heart of hearts my first baby would be a girl? This feeling had been with me through the whole pregnancy. So even though people at my party were saying things like, 'Charlotte really wants a girl – she'll go mad if it's a boy!' it wasn't even an issue because (a) I felt sure it was a girl, and (b) I would have genuinely been happy whatever it was, as long as it was healthy. Imagine a cute little version of Jake with big ears?!! Yet, I was overcome with this intuition. I knew from the moment I was pregnant that I was having a girl. Also, I was so, so, so sick and people say that happens with girls more than boys . . .

OK, I admit I was a *tiny* bit nervous when the plane flew over our heads, just in case blue smoke came out. At first the plane was making these moves in the air and nothing was coming out, which made everyone really confused. I was thinking, 'They're dragging it out here!' Suddenly it just started going pink and everyone screamed. Then the sky-writer started to draw a heart and everyone thought he was spelling out the baby's name! But as the heart became clear and pink confetti was launched from a cannon all over us, I was in raptures. (The funniest thing was that Elton John was performing about twenty minutes down the road and I saw people tweeting that you could see this plane flying overhead mid-concert and everyone saw the heart. I'd managed to upstage Elton John at his own gig. What a result!)

I was over the moon and couldn't stop smiling and hugging

everyone. Everyone was so overjoyed for us, and Mam was screaming because she honestly thought it was a boy. Sophie and Holly were shrieking and jumping about – everyone was just so happy. The whole night felt like a scene from a movie, it was so magical. Me and Jake were standing at the front, and we had so many people we loved around us. It was honestly such a wonderful moment.*

*Oh my God. Just as I'm writing this a pigeon has flown into the window of my living room and slid down the glass! I need to stop having such clean windows because birds keep thinking they can just fly right into it – it's so reflective it looks like trees! I'm turning into a bird murderer without even meaning to. Shit, I can't cope with the stress levels! My hormones are bad enough as it is without worrying about wildlife flying at the house. I think I need a lie down.

And while I'm there I'm going to google how to bring pigeons back to life . . .

8

My baby is . . .

a big surprise for the Geordie Shore OGs

During those first months of my pregnancy we were filming *Geordie Shore: The Reunion 2022*, which was going to be on MTV around the time the baby was due. It was a whole different experience to when I was previously on the show! Luckily, I was able to announce my pregnancy right at the beginning, otherwise it would have been so hard to pretend to be mortal all the time.

As I've said, I wanted to break the news of my pregnancy to my absolute best friends Sophie and Holly in a really special way, so I'd agreed with the producers that they'd film me telling them as part of *The Reunion*. It took so much planning but it was SO worth it. I knew the fans of the show wanted to see the moment they found out because it was such an important part of my *Geordie Shore* journey. But I can't tell you how hard it was keeping it from the two people who knew me better than anyone, especially Sophie who was on to me and asking me questions every time I saw her. So when the time came to reveal the truth I was beside myself with excitement.

I planned the whole thing with the producers. I invited Sophie and Holly to stay at mine for a sleepover the night before we were all due to meet the others for the big reunion. They thought we were just there to be filmed reminiscing and gossiping about what was to come. But I knew otherwise!

All the cameras were set and they came over to mine. 'My sisters have arrived!' I shouted excitedly. I began by trying to throw them off the scent, asking about what they thought was going to happen and who was coming. We were chatting about who we thought would be there from the show – and they started taking the piss, saying I used to fancy Greg! I then showed them a memory book that I'd made in the lead-up to the reunion (I do love a good memory book). What they didn't realise was that at the end of the book, I'd planted a very special surprise.

The book opened with pictures of us all from the very beginning of the show. Nothing could have prepared us for what *Geordie Shore* was going to be. We felt like rock stars when we were on the show – we basically did what every other person did at that age, except ours all happened on a TV show. Looking back made us get emotional, remembering just how special our friendships are and how we'd be nothing without them, or the show. I would feel absolutely devastated if I didn't have these girls in my life.

They flicked through the memory book and got to the last page. I said to them, 'I've saved the best one for last.' They looked at the picture – it was a scan of my baby – and they looked back in shock, 'NO WAY!'

There were so many tears. They were both so amazed, but they were just in bits and overjoyed for me. We hugged each other so hard and then I showed them my bump and they were jumping up and down excitedly, saying how proud of me they were. That moment felt so special. When I'd left *Geordie Shore* after the ectopic pregnancy I didn't even know if I'd be able to have a baby. So, to sit there on the bed with Sophie and Holly – my 'day ones' – and to be going back into the show with a baby in my belly was an incredible feeling. I made them swear to secrecy because then I was going to tell everyone else from the show at the *Reunion* filming.

Sophie had been a bit apprehensive about taking part in the reunion at first and kept asking me, 'Have I taken two steps forward and now two steps back?' I think she felt that she'd left for a reason and now she wanted people to know her as she really is, not the *Geordie Shore* version of Sophie. It wasn't always a given that I was going to go back into *Geordie Shore* either. Not because I don't love the show – because I absolutely do. I always, *always* said that, if there was a reunion, I would go back. For me it wouldn't be about the drinking or the partying, it would be more about coming back together to resolve old feuds and bury hatchets. And because *Geordie Shore* made us who we are, and we need to be eternally grateful for everything that it's given us. I thought, 'I will always be there for what the show needs, because I feel like I owe it to the show.' But – and I feel awful saying this – the show changed a lot after we left. There were new characters who joined, all of the OGs had gone, and it wasn't the same format and same personalities. So, my only reservation about doing the reunion show was that I truly believed it needed to be a proper reunion – not bringing people back I've never met. I felt like I wanted my reunion show to be people like Sophie, Holly, Gary, Vicky, James, Jay, Greg and Becca – all the people who made *Geordie Shore* what it was from the very early series. Just like going to school reunion – you wouldn't go to one where there were different people from a different year! I think (I hope) original fans of the show will understand what I mean by that. No disrespect to any of the new people who were on the show more recently – but I just felt it needed to be core cast members. The OGs!

One of my favourite parts of filming the reunion was getting ready in a room in Newcastle with Sophie and Holly. We didn't know who we were going to see or what it would be like. Sophie was absolutely shitting herself that her ex, Joel Corry, was going to be there! That made us laugh so much. Who'd have thought back then that Joel would end up being more famous than her and this massive superstar DJ! It's mad that wherever she goes on holiday there are billboards with his face on! It's a good job she's not bitter, as it would be a horrendous reminder to see your ex's picture plastered everywhere you go! I think there was a part of her that wanted to see him to say a proper well done. She has a lot of love for him and she's proud of him. She also kept saying, 'I look good at the minute,' and if there's ever a time to see your ex, it's when you look amazing!

There were so many old faces who returned in the end. People were all going through different emotions – having to confront their old loves and people they'd not seen for years. There was Marnie and Aaron . . . Holly and Kyle . . . and old friends who had fallen out who thought they'd never speak again. It was like one big therapy session in the end – a chance to air all those demons and get things out in the open.

When I saw all the others on camera for the first time, we were shooting in this cold warehouse bar. I was feeling so ill, and I kept throwing up in the toilet – I had to pretend I had the shits! I was also pretending I was drinking from this glass of prosecco while everyone else was getting pissed out of their heads. It was so amazing to see everyone, but I got freaked right out when Marnie, who was pregnant with her second baby, started moaning about how her boobs had changed from pregnancy. She showed me one of her nipples and it was MASSIVE and really dark! What was about to happen to me??!

I really tried hard not to let being pregnant ruin my *Geordie Shore* experience or make me suddenly seem boring.

There was one time when we were all away in Portugal when I nearly did a twenty-two-hour day of filming! I'd told myself I had to go to the nightclub with everyone else. I was so tired but I had to do it. But what a change from my old times on *Geordie Shore*! There were still people necking off around me, while I was really missing Jake – I couldn't call him because we didn't have our phones apart from one hour a day. At one point when we were back at the house, I was slumped on a chair thinking, 'I want to be back in my baby bubble with Jake, googling stuff for the nursery!'

New beginnings, old memories

I looked at Holly when we were in Portugal and thought about what a journey she had come on since being on *Geordie Shore*. When I think about the beginning of the series and what she was like – such a shut-off person compared to now – it's actually quite sad to recall, because back then she was lost. She is younger than me and I remember being quite shocked when she came in as she would always be wearing literally five pairs of eyelashes. But it was her mask. Holly readily admits that herself now. On the other hand, I was there rolling around pissing myself in the bed and not caring what anyone thought of me. But it's comforting to know that I somehow helped her back then because she grew more confident by my side, and she's now completely and utterly her brilliant self. So even though my behaviour wasn't exactly that of a traditional 'role model' – *I mean, I haven't been teaching people about eco friendliness!* – it makes me proud when girls send me kind messages telling me that I've helped them be more like them, and NOT GIVE SO MUCH OF A SHIT! I live my life as a free spirit and I don't think I'll ever change, I'm glad about that. When I'm eighty I'll probably still be getting torn apart for something just because I'm living my best life.

Holly looked unreal during filming *Geordie Shore: The Reunion* and I remember looking at her in her bikini one day in Portugal and thinking that all the boys fancied her. It was such a transformation and turnaround – she'd gone from being unlucky in love to getting engaged to a lovely guy called Jacob who she was about to marry . . . and now she had all of her exes falling at her feet. James – who had a history with her from years ago in the show – stared at her gobsmacked and just mouthed, 'I so would!' And who wouldn't?! Of course, James was nothing compared to Kyle. Kyle really affected Holly and had made her feel so shit because he just didn't want to be in a relationship when they were together, but she'd been completely besotted. He's so lovely though and has grown up so much since all those years ago he now has a family of his own. It was good to see him and Holly air their differences once and for all. Their skeletons came out good and proper and the demons between the pair of them were well and truly exorcised.

We all went to Ibiza for Holly's wedding. Sophie and I were bridesmaids and it was so special. We were all in really grown-up places in our lives now – and it was so nice to see. I was pregnant. Holly was getting married. Aaron was having another baby. Marnie was having another baby. So many major new milestones!

Jake was there as a guest too, which made it even more perfect. I was feeling ill most of the day so I couldn't party like I used to – I ended up going to bed early. But this was the first time Jake had met all my *Geordie Shore* lot and they had the best time – I did get a bit jealous at some points when they were downing shots. I was so glad Jake mingled and got to know them. Once again, he proved to be unlike any other boyfriend I'd ever had. He can be thrown into any situation and hold his own and just be brilliant.

As I watched Holly walk down the aisle I was thinking, 'Wow, we are watching our sister getting married!' Here we all are in Ibiza, the place we used to PARTY PARTY PARTY! If someone had told us all those years ago – when we were in bed, hungover, with sick down our faces and no pants on – that Holly would be the first of the OGs to get married and me and Sophie would be bridesmaids, we would never ever have believed them. Not one person back then would have guessed that this is how our lives would end up. And now Holly's a wife! I can still feel that moment. I'd never witnessed a more beautiful wedding – they said their own vows and it was so personal. Sophie and I bawled our eyes out during the whole ceremony.

Sophie is convinced she's psychic – she says she sees an image when she thinks the boy is *the one*. Sophie said that when Holly first met Jacob, her husband, she knew instantly that they were meant to be. She also said the same when she met Jake. She told me, 'I can see your future – he is your man!' Standing next to her at the wedding I thought, 'I hope you find someone soon too.' Since then she has met a lovely guy, Jordan. I hope he's *the one*. Now she's chilled out a bit more I think this could be it. There, that's *my* psychic ability kicking in now!

To absent friends

The big question around the series had always been whether Gary and Vicky would turn up. They were a core part of the original show – if it was going to be about the OGs, they needed to be there.

I think deep down we all knew that Vicky wouldn't come back. Greg told us that he'd spoken to her and asked her advice about whether he should do it himself and she'd said, 'Yes – just do it!' She just didn't want to be part of it herself as she felt that she'd moved on. Vicky was never going to do *The Reunion*. She doesn't even seem to want to be associated with the show. Ever since she left, she's had a whole reboot of the person that she was on the show and completely changed.

Whereas we were all really happy to be part of it. I think she didn't like the person she was on the show, and now feels a bit like she must prove to people she's not that person.

Holly said that she didn't think Vicky would want to come back and have the conversations that needed to be had. She felt that there were issues that needed to be brought up, such as her not being that nice to her at the start. But I pointed out that she did always have your back when she was on your side. As I think I've said before, we've never openly had an argument or a fight. There's never been a massive fall-out. We just don't speak. The press did whip stuff up between us a bit though, and I do admit that I gloated a bit when the sales of my fitness DVD trebled hers! But that's just my competitive streak! I also remember a sad time quite a long time ago when a mutual friend of ours died; I reached out to her in a text and she replied with a really nice simple message back. We've never had this huge row like the press make out – we're just very different people.

But we all hoped Gary would turn up. And everyone else was really angry that he didn't. We thought he might come, at least just for one night. And he had loads of opportunities too. We had the first night, the holiday in Portugal and a house party at the end. I texted him and got no reply. Gary used to love *Geordie Shore*, it was his life. It's not like just because he's a parent he couldn't meet up with people he'd done so much with and celebrate it. *Geordie Shore* gave him so much. He wouldn't be where he is without it. Everyone was so pissed off

130

at him. The producers didn't even know what was going on as he'd made out he was coming at one point.

Gary doesn't even talk to any of us any more. He used to be mates with Holly and Sophie for a while and then he cut them off too. Holly was absolutely devastated that he didn't contact her and didn't do the show. We would not have been where we are without *Geordie Shore*. We felt it was only right to go back and thank the show for what it did for us. It was a dead reflective time, it was really nice to think how far we'd come. And Gary missed out.

I also wanted to be able to share my news with him as he had been such a part of my past. I wanted him to be happy for me, bearing in mind everything I went through with the ectopic pregnancy. When he'd got his girlfriend Emma pregnant, I'd congratulated them on Twitter. That was really hard. It was a difficult time for me because I hadn't long had the ectopic pregnancy and I was dealing with a lot of sad things. And then there was one night when we all saw each other at Aaron's boxing match, and I told Emma how glowing she looked. I thought we were all good and fine. There was no animosity, I thought everything in the past had moved on.

Even though Gary didn't show for the reunion, I still half expected to hear from him once the news of my pregnancy was out. He knew I was pregnant – it was all over the press when I announced it – but where were my congratulations? He couldn't even say it back to me. I was the one who went through all the shit, I was the one who could have died. He is a father, he knows what it's like to have a family. He could have said he was happy for me. He used to say, 'I love Charlotte, even as a friend, I will always be there for her.' So where was my message? He didn't even have to do it publicly, he could have done it in private. It would have meant the absolute world to hear that he was happy for me after all that had happened. Just one message.

The girls and I have decided that in eight years' time we would like to do it all again – *The Twenty-Year Geordie Shore Reunion*. It will be like *The Real Housewives of the North East*.

If I'm honest, it was a bit weird Jake watching *Geordie Shore: The Reunion*. I don't know what I thought it was going to be like. I knew what I'd filmed for it but I didn't think they'd play as many old clips as they did. And that's what was awkward. When the first episode aired in September, I was tweeting about it and getting really excited. Me and Jake sat and watched it together, because he obviously wanted to support me. But there were so many clips of me and Gary . . . and I wanted to hide. But Jake was still so composed and cool about it; he can't have loved seeing it, but he's so mature he didn't kick off. Now, if that had been any of my ex-boyfriends seeing me on TV with an old boyfriend in that way there would have been a screaming match, one of us would have thrown something or been kicked out of the house – it would have been carnage. We would be finished. That's how pathetic my old relationships were. Jake took it in his stride and said he always understood that *Geordie Shore* was a certain type of show. And he knew that me and Gary were a huge part of the whole narrative.

When the first episode ended I said, 'I don't think it's all going to be like that . . .!'

And he said, 'Don't worry, I get it – but maybe just watch the rest of the show on your own!'

9

My baby is . . .

a girl who's going to learn to deal with trolls

Now that I'm a mam, the whole idea of social media and trolling feels like a much bigger deal. Even though I've dealt with it all of the time I've been in the public eye – the thought of anyone ever saying anything bad about her absolutely floors me. I feel so protective of anything negative hurting my daughter that I am hoping (and manifesting!) that social media gets wiped out forever. Or at least there being some serious troll-police so bullies can't hide behind their screens without there being consequences.

When I meet people for the first time, one of the most common questions I get asked is, 'How do you deal with the trolls?' Because if I had a pound for every time someone used to tell me my lips were too big or my face looked like a piece of plastic, I'd be so rich I'd be practically pooing out money. I've talked about this in the past and said I've learnt not to think about the haters, and not to give them any oxygen. Everyone is always going to have an opinion of you and you cannot change that. Not everyone is going to love you and it's easier all round if you just come to terms with that. I also have the opinion that if the criticism is coming from someone I don't know then quite frankly, why give a fuck about them?

There are some awfully mean people out there in the world. And while I don't like to acknowledge the negatives I do have to laugh sometimes.

> I'm at a point where I can't tell the difference between @charlottegshore and @caitlinjenner

I've been compared to a lot of people. But the main one that people say about me is that I'm Michael Jackson. Type my name and MJ's into Google and there are thousands of comparisons. I am literally the King of Pop. I sometimes say that when my work all dries up I will just have to become a Michael Jackson tribute act. Me mam now gets people saying *she* looks like Caitlin Jenner – so when I told her about this tweet she said, 'How dare they? Don't they know who I am?!' So now she calls me MJ and I call her Caitlin!

What I find the most bizarre is that any bad comments always seem to come from men. My friend Craig, the head guy at MTV who I'm dead close with, is always looking at the social comments about us girls on *Geordie Shore* and he says, 'It's always blokes who seem to lay into you guys and I don't understand it.' These are grown men who probably have kids – *daughters*! – of their own. I feel like I can understand it with girls a bit more, because they sometimes get jealous and give bitchy comments. But when I think about some men, sitting at home typing on the computer about a young girl?! That is the least gentlemanly thing I have ever witnessed. I've called some of them out for it before, because I think they should be ashamed of themselves. I wonder how they would feel if someone was saying that kind of thing about their children?

I went on the red carpet once at the *National Television Awards* with this lovely dress on – I felt so glam. I get really anxious going on red carpets but I thought that I looked like a movie star, so I posted a photo on my Twitter. And there was a man (who probably had a family) who replied and just said I looked plastic and hideous. WHY IS IT ALWAYS MEN?? It's getting very boring now!

Social media, and the way technology is always changing, can be amazing and horrendous in equal measure. I've always been obsessed with it though. I like to get in there and be involved because if you don't jump on the bandwagon, you get left behind. I love technology. I love how the world's changing so rapidly. In years to come, jobs and everything are going to be so different because of social media. But there are pros and cons in social media, like there are pros and cons in life.

It's not just trolling on social media though – bullying happens all the way through life. In school, you get the stupid times where people might call you ugly, or you get negativity from the class bully – that's something you must deal with and try not to let it get to you. School bullying was way worse than any trolling I've ever received so I developed a thick skin early on! I was called Goofy and every name under the sun, and believe me it was tough going into school every day wondering what I was going to get called today, face to face, with no escaping it.

With social media you can block people, you can disable your comments, you can go to your settings and actually type in words that you don't want to ever show on your Instagram. So if I wanted I could type in 'nose', and then no one could comment about my nose ever again. There are so many controls that you can use. I think people need to educate themselves more on the controls, and then maybe the trolling wouldn't bother them because they just wouldn't see it. I don't have to read articles about me and certainly I don't have to read the comments.

Also, when it comes to online, whenever there are nasty comments there will also be a load of nice, positive comments. I'm the type of person who wants to focus on the positives. For every person saying I look like a duck face, there's also someone saying that I'm so beautiful, that I make them laugh and I've helped them get through low points in life. And that's what I try to focus on, rather than the stupid, ridiculous comments someone else has made. Everyone needs to stop dwelling on the negatives and notice the nice things people say. I've never wanted to walk away from what I do, because I get thousands of comments every week from people telling me I've made their week. I post a photo and someone will say, 'You look beautiful, you're glowing.' So I just try not to let trolls mess with my life.

Saying that, it's also none of anyone's business what you do to your face or body! I honestly don't see the problem in things like getting your nose done because you don't like the shape of it. When I was younger, I had bad teeth, so me mam made me get braces to sort them out. She didn't want me to grow up with crooked teeth because that's not nice. SO, WHAT IS THE DIFFERENCE? How is a mother sorting their child out with a better smile any different to a grown adult paying to have her nose corrected and the bump in it taken off? It's still a cosmetic procedure! It took me five years to decide about the rhinoplasty but the kind of stick I got for being honest about that was horrendous. I had one TV appearance when I felt really backed into a corner about my decision being awful. And then the next week, I saw men on *This Morning* talking about hair transplants and being applauded for their bravery speaking about something they were insecure about. The contrast between how a woman is treated and a man is sickening.

Big deal! It's my body!

Being so open about what I've had done is a double-edged

sword, because you open yourself up to criticism. I've always been honest about having my boobs corrected from the 'uni-boob' (congenital symmastia) after being trolled for the way they look. (And yes, I had implants put in at the same time, but I've since had them removed because one side became impacted and they were too big!) I know so many people who go out of their way to keep every single thing they've had done hidden and I think, 'Why would you want to lie about it?' But sometimes I look at it and almost wish I'd done the same. But I realise I'm a huge influence on a lot of people, and I have to be honest. It's also my nature – I just hate liars!

But over the last year or so, my outlook has changed and I have come to realise that the trolling is NOT OK. Just because I'm in the public eye it doesn't mean I'm fair game. There was a shocking moment when it all came to a crescendo – I don't even really know how to describe what happened, but it was like a media frenzy and sort of an attack.

My face in the firing line

In April 2021 Channel 5 aired a show called *Celebrities: What Happened To Your Face?* It was literally just a bunch of people tearing me apart on a TV show. And looking back now, it was such a huge, overwhelming thing to go through. My agent, Kate, had accidentally heard about the show a few months before it came out. I think the production company had asked another of the agency's clients for a comment about me. In this day and age, with mental health being so much more talked about, she was shocked that it was even being considered in the first place. So naturally she said to them, 'This sounds totally unethical!' Emails went back and forth, and, when she heard nothing more, she thought it wasn't going ahead.

And then all of a sudden we started seeing it advertised on TV and I remember thinking, 'What is even happening?' I'm so used to my looks being pulled apart every single day that I'd learnt to build up a really thick skin. I just thought that was part of being famous. But this was something else. It looked as if the show was focused on me, but there were other celebs who were being talked about too – like Sylvester Stallone, Madonna and Simon Cowell. They were literally the most famous people you can ever imagine. At one point I just shrugged and thought, 'Oh well, at least I'm in esteemed company! Yes, I've had my nose and lips done but I've spoken about that. Out of all the others they could have chosen – even people who have had about 75,000 facelifts – they chose me. Maybe it's a compliment?' I was trying to look at the positives again.

I saw a few ads for it and thought I'd just ignore it. I wasn't going to watch it. But on the night it aired, I suddenly had all these people messaging me on Instagram and texting me. The first one was a family friend who sent me a WhatsApp saying, 'Charlotte, this is disgusting. I can't believe there is a TV show like this about you.' Then my friend Terry sent me one, 'I cannot believe this is on!' I started to get more and more messages. I began to get anxious – it must have been really bad if it was getting this reaction. What was being said about me? Then Holly started on her Insta stories – she was kicking off about how bad it was and telling people they should complain to Ofcom. So I thought I'd better watch it. I turned on the TV and it was really bad. There were so-called experts on there, laying into my face, saying stuff about my cheeks and that I'd had filler (I've never had filler in my life). One woman said, 'She's getting visible signs of having fillers. Good jobs are not visible, bad jobs are extremely visible. You can see her lips are too full, the apple of her cheek is too big, almost like a golf ball. That's looking slightly unreal.' Then another said, 'In my professional opinion I think she looks better and more herself before she had all this done. They've taken a bit of what we call a cookie-cutter approach to filling her face where they don't respect the natural anatomy. I wouldn't advise that she continue filling because it's going to age her face.' It went on and on. I had to turn it off in the end.

But I was getting more and more messages – Twitter was exploding about it. Holly was enraged and was reposting messages from her followers who were equally furious. I was so shocked about the fact that these people *really cared*. I could not believe it. And although everyone was defending me, I started panicking because my instant reaction was that this show was going to encourage more trolls and more bad comments about my looks. I thought I was going to wake up to my face all over the papers, with them saying I looked plastic and like Michael Jackson again. Eventually I managed to go to sleep.

In the morning my phone was on fire with more messages. But instead of opening up social media to see the front pages of the papers with some hideous commentary on me, I had thousands of messages of support. They were from all sorts of people, all walks of life, some in really high-up positions. People I'd never met in my life were saying how vile the show was, that it was wrong and I didn't deserve it. I was so overwhelmed, I just cried all that day. I think the biggest thing that hit me was the fact that all this time I'd been believing I had to accept this sort of criticism and that I deserved it. But there were over 7,000 complaints to Ofcom and loads of journalists were asking for comment. It made me realise, for the first time, that actually I AM entitled to some self-worth and self-care. It occurred to me that *maybe* I was allowed to stick up for myself. It just showed me that the world is actually changing. People shouldn't stand for this treatment or bullying or behaviour any more. It's just not cool. I was sobbing and sobbing, reading all the messages of support – everyone was so kind. Kate was upset for me too, she felt it was so wrong. The show was a huge turning point for me. And I got really fired up. If I accepted this then other people might think they deserved bad things being said about them too. When is enough enough? Just because we're in the public eye, doesn't mean we aren't human. Fortunately, I'm strong enough to deal with it, but many aren't! I knew I had to say something. I had to acknowledge it in some way. So, I put a statement up on my Instagram:

I cannot quite believe I am saying this but here goes. Last night, Channel 5 & Crackit Productions put out a one-hour documentary called *Celebrities – What Happened To Your Face – Charlotte Crosby*.

In 2021 a main UK channel & production company believed it would be a good use of airtime to dissect my physical appearance.

I have seen how many of you saw it, switched off & complained – many not even 'fans' of me, just good people who know right from wrong. Thank you for that, and for your messages of love and support.

I am aware I have put myself and my face in the public eye. TV and broadcasting has given me and my family a life we could never have dreamed of. I enjoy it, am enormously grateful for it and many of my respected closest friends work within the industry.

I have had a public battle with my appearance, and had to go through personal trauma & issues of self-confidence in the spot-light. I like to think I'm an honest, balanced person – I get it, I understand the interest.

One quick google or look at my Instagram page, you'll see how intensely I've been targeted by trolls, and how I've learnt to ignore the hate, focus on the positives and work on living myself again. It's a process, it's taken time, compassion, personal & professional support.

At a time when the broadcast & media world were backing a policy of 'be kind', Channel 5 & Crackit decided to commission this 1 hour special on 'rubber lip Charlotte' (their words not mine.)

Their 'experts' dissected my 'plastic face' with disgust, discussing my fluctuating weight (with images), and then decided to flash up the worst troll comments from the past 5–6 years.

I want to say here for context. When this was commissioned last March 2020, my agent found out about it & was appalled. She very clearly outlined to Crackit Productions not just how immoral and insensitive it was but how detrimental this would be to my mental health. They ignored her, despite repeated correspondence, and ran with it regardless. We only found out this week when it was in the TV Listings that it was still going ahead – unbelievable.

Dealing with trolls is one thing, you ignore, you block. BUT where are we as a society, when the trolls are on the mainstream TV channels? Will they now take responsibility for my dip in mental health and my plummeted self-esteem? Do they take responsibility for the resulting press from the show, again discussing how 'shocking' my face is? Channel 5 have a list of mental health helplines on their website – is this for viewers, or the subjects of their poor choice in programming like me? Broadcasters are so keen to do psych tests for shows, yet at the same time give space to programmes which destroy the mental health of its subjects.

That hour could have been used to host a mental health documentary. That hour could have educated the public in the many issues & good causes which need publicity. That hour didn't need to go after a 31 year old woman for her appearance, choices and 'rubber lips'.

When is enough enough? Just because we're in the public eye, doesn't mean we aren't human. Fortunately I'm strong enough to deal with it but many aren't.

I got an apology in the end from the TV company and the show will never be seen again. It had been a massive moment for me, and I felt really proud that I'd said something and stuck up for myself. I now knew I didn't deserve all that kind of shit. I felt really empowered.

Unbelievably though, when I thought the press had forgotten about it, I was reminded of the whole thing all over again. I got COVID the following New Year and there was story about me in the paper that said, 'Charlotte Crosby breaks down in tears in emotional social media clip as she's forced to isolate on New Year's Eve following positive COVID test.' Next to the headline was a photo of me crying. Was the photo of me crying about catching COVID? NO! It was a photo from when I'd been crying with happiness because some people had been nice to me after the documentary! How on earth is that allowed in the media?? It's fake news! Yes, I was a bit gutted about cancelling my New Year plans, but I definitely wasn't sobbing my eyes out! I was actually thinking, 'This is good because I can start the new year without a hangover!' I was shocked at how they had just manipulated it to look like I had cried about missing New Year's Eve when I hadn't! And because it looked like I was being a stupid bitch, loads of readers then started writing hateful comments underneath the article saying, 'Get a grip, Charlotte, we all have COVID – move on! Isolate just like all the rest of us do!'

It's baffling that people are still so hooked on the way we look. There are so many people in this world who say, 'It's all about what's on the inside and you have to stop judging people by their looks.' But no one seems to be living by that. There's still a constant obsession with what people have done to their faces.

When I first went on *Geordie Shore* I was actually really pretty. I was dead slim and wore nice clothes. I thought my lips were a little bit thin, but that was it. (Admittedly my eyebrows were a bit on the thin side too, but I think we all went through that stage back in the day. Luckily those kinds of trends change.) I wasn't really bothered about my looks back then. Then I started putting weight on, drinking too much and losing it a bit. When I look back on that time, I feel like I really let myself go and I shouldn't have done. My style really went downhill then too, I was wearing the most ridiculous, awful things – anything baggy that covered me up. I basically wore different coloured tents every day. I had an oversized shirt-dress in about seventy-five different colours. I wore that all the time because I felt so fat.

But I think it's important to remember in life that nothing is ever a constant – everyone grows and changes. Obviously, as previously discussed, I've had my nose job, and boobs in and boobs out – but that's just because I had those things available to me. I actually think if I hadn't been on TV I wouldn't have had those things done. I wouldn't have had a nose job because I wouldn't have been seeing it in front of me the whole time. It wouldn't be this lumpy reminder. But I guess that's the same for all young girls now because with social media they're constantly reminded of their flaws.

When I look in the mirror now, I'm not even joking, but I think I'm bloody gorgeous! I honestly don't ever look at myself and see the things that people write online. I feel very lucky that all the trolling hasn't got to me so much that it's affected my confidence. Also I'm fortunate that Jake is so lovely about me and makes me feel so special. Even though I have a lazy eye he says my eyes are beautiful and he loves them!

I have a list of rules to help me deal with any negativity. Hopefully they might help you too.

Charlotte's rules for dealing with trolls,
when you're in the public eye

1. Remember you don't know these people. They do not know you. And you don't know them.
2. Don't give a shit about a stranger – obviously if the negativity is coming from your best friend, your boyfriend or your family, then you might think, 'Oh shit, maybe I'm doing something wrong.' But these people don't matter!
3. Someone somewhere is always slagging you off, but that's because they feel shit about themselves.
4. Honestly, I think you can do a few deep breaths and say to yourself, 'Fuck you,' then smile and blow yourself a kiss in the mirror.
5. Letting it bother you is giving trolls exactly what they want.
6. Never react to it – because then they have won.
7. You are an individual. You don't dress for anyone else. You dress for you. You brush your hair for you. You put make-up on for you. You don't need to answer to anyone else.

Even though I am happy with my looks, during pregnancy I felt like a big piece of poo. Some women seem to love being pregnant and everyone talks about them being glowing. But my God, my body was not prepared for what was to come. I thought I'd be walking around looking beautiful and healthy and stylish. But I felt like a lump of shit that gets rolled around across the floor like a dung beetle. I couldn't even get myself around – I had to be pushed about by a dung beetle! I felt so ill and so tired. I couldn't wait to have my energy back and be normal again. (I also was fed up of the taste of Gaviscon – I was getting through bottles of it because the heartburn was so bad.)

Thankfully I had my personal trainers for the app keeping me active a bit – I had no choice! Once my baby news was out in the open, we devised some really good workout plans to help other people who were in pregnancy. And it actually made it fun to work out. Sarah, the coach, came up with a plan where I had to sit on the bouncy ball with weights and I found I actually had a really good time.

I probably wasn't putting in as much work as I should. Sarah was also pregnant and she was insane – she was due in three weeks and she was still doing all these mad classes at the gym!

I didn't want to get obsessed with my fitness though – because I can be a bit of an obsessive person. I wanted to just let my body do its thing. But after the baby was born I was determined that I would get back into my good routines. I was never going to give up on exercise because I usually like the feeling you get from it – when you feel you can literally conquer the world.

*   *   *

I think it's so important that people feel good about them-selves, and ignore the things people say and just be confident in who they are. So my message to my baby girl is this: you shouldn't ever have to put up with people criticising you or how you look. And you shouldn't feel pressure to conform, put make-up on, look a certain way because it's more 'accept-able' either. Whatever you want to do to your hair, your body or yourself – it's up to YOU! Don't try to copy others either – because being your original self makes you so much more special. There is nobody else on this earth who is you with your looks and personality and your way of thinking. So just own that. Don't get caught up in the whole 'I want to look a certain way all the time'. There's nothing special about trying to be like everyone else. You're born your original self and that's who you are meant to be.

My Pregnancy Make-Up Routine

I found that when I became pregnant my skin became dead sensitive and started reacting differently to the products that I'd always used before – even a make-up wipe! So here's the routine I had when I was pregnant and I've kept now because it's lighter and you can wear it every day:

1. Foundation – Milani's foundation is actually something I had used pre-pregnancy. I needed something light because my face looked weird with too much make-up when I was pregnant. What did we ever do before beauty blenders were a thing? I don't know!

2. Next, concealer – I made some new discoveries for concealer. First was Hourglass in the shade 'Beech', and second was Laura Mercier Flawless Fusion shade '2.5W'. They both have ingredients that are good for the skin and don't dry it. I blended them with a brush. I needed extra coverage under the eyes because I wasn't sleeping as much as before.

3. Then eyebrows – Benefit Precisely My Brow is dead thick so the precision on it is amazing. I'm not that good at my eyebrows if I'm honest – I just scribble them on!

4. So, for contouring – Charlotte Tilbury Filmstar Bronze & Glow palette in 'Medium to Deep', just for some bone structure on the face. I always dab over it with a bit of powder after, I don't like it looking too heavy now I'm a mam!

5. Blusher – I like a powder such as Benefit Sugarbomb. Dip the brush in the pinky bits and it gives your cheeks a rosy glow. I also like a bit of pink on the tip of my nose. Although make sure it doesn't look too much like Rudolph.

6. Lips – I found a nice one from Charlotte Tilbury again in a shade called 'Yes Honey', which is a browny, toffee colour and it's really nice (I've had a lot of compliments about it). I'll also add some 'Iconic Nude' lipliner beforehand.

7. Eyes – there's also this amazing thing from Charlotte Tilbury called Hollywood Exagger-Eyes Liner Duo – one bit is for the inner eye and makes them look wider and brighter, and the other end is a darker eyeliner which I put on the top lid because I always have patches where I pull my eyelashes out.

8. Lashes – my favourite lashes are called Tatti Lashes, which look identical to when you get eyelash extensions. They are so nice and wispy and are a game changer.

So that's it – my lightweight pregnancy and new mam make-up face. I know I'm not a make-up artist and I have limited skills but I wanted to share some handy ideas because if I can do them – anyone can!

I don't know how to do eyeshadow, so I usually leave that bit. And I have no eyelashes or real hair – but apparently everything grows better in pregnancy which I was quite excited about. Although I was a bit worried that would mean my pubes would start sprouting massively too, which wouldn't have been ideal. But hell, I'd take it like a woman if that's what's meant to be.

10

My baby is . . .

the best excuse for a holiday and ANOTHER party!

With Mam's surgery over we were all starting to feel like we could get excited about the baby again and plan things as a family. Although Mam had her chemo looming, it was nowhere near as scary a thought as not knowing what was ahead had been. Jake was now such a part of all of our worlds – none of us could ever remember what we did without him in our lives. He was loving living in Crosby Manor and we were preparing the place for our daughter and trying to get our heads around parenthood. It was all very grown up indeed. But we knew we needed to make the most of being a couple too, so we decided to do one last big holiday.

No milkshake in Mauritius

God knows why on earth we chose to go all the way to Mauritius for our babymoon, but we did. Going on an eleven-hour flight when you're heavily pregnant probably isn't the greatest idea.

I think I was about twenty-eight weeks pregnant, so I checked with Mr Okaro that I could still fly, and he said it was OK. But the journey was ridiculously uncomfortable with my massive bump. We had a connecting flight to Paris, and then flew from there to Mauritius. So I was hobbling around the airport in Paris, waiting for the connecting flight, thinking, 'Why do I do this? I bring it on myself. Why do I have to always go too far? It's pathetic!'

Then, when we landed in Mauritius we were disappointed with our hotel. I was a bit of a diva about it, I've got to admit – but I was tired and hormonal. Something just wasn't right. We hadn't really done our research properly, but when we'd booked it, we just thought it looked super special and a sort of nice luxury place to go. We'd been travelling about twenty hours by the time we arrived because of having to change in Paris and then having an hour and a half drive from the airport. We pulled up in our hire car at the hotel and it was quite old fashioned – and by old fashioned, I basically mean old. We were in the reception hall and there were these glass windows with nothing behind them – like there had been shops in there before but now all that was left was these empty shells, all run down, dusty and abandoned. It felt really desolate. I thought, 'This is strange.' We got taken to our bedroom which was also a bit old fashioned but nothing that bad that I would have moaned about it – there were a few stains on the furniture and marks where people had left their cups, a bit like the cleaner had just given up halfway through her shift.

On the way to Mauritius, we'd had our sun cream and my new bottle of Gaviscon taken off us because they were too big for hand luggage. I really needed both badly. I had to have sunblock because your skin goes so weird and sensitive when you're pregnant. And I needed more Gaviscon because my heartburn was through the roof – it was horrendous! So, we said, 'Let's just go to the shop and then sit round the pool and have a nice drink and chill instead.'

We got to the hotel shop and the shelves were empty, so I asked, 'Have you got any sun cream or sunblock?'

And they replied, 'No, we have nothing.'

'Where should I go to get some sun cream then? I'm pregnant, so I need a really high factor.'

The assistant just pointed out the door of the hotel. Well, having already travelled an hour and a half to get there, we knew there were no shops just round the corner – it was more like a load of plants and forests! There was *nothing* nearby. This was a five-star hotel so I just presumed it would have stuff.

By this time, we were so tired, and I just wanted to get in the pool. I decided I'd just have to sit by the pool under an umbrella for now; Jake had a factor 30 so that would have to do for the time being.

Now, seeing as I couldn't *drink* drink, I'd become very partial to a strawberry milkshake since being pregnant. And it always seemed to help a bit with the heartburn and soothe me. So, on the way to the pool, I stopped at the bar and ordered a random beer for Jake and said, 'I'll have a strawberry milkshake please.'

The barman looked at me blankly. 'We don't have strawberry milkshakes.'

Oh. 'I don't mind if I have to go over to the restaurant to get it,' I offered.

But no, that wasn't going to happen either. 'We do not do strawberry milkshakes in this hotel.'

I was watching him making a piña colada and I thought, 'Hang on, if you can make a piña colada surely you can make a strawberry milkshake??'

I was just so fed up. I wanted to have a good time and relax and enjoy our last holiday together before the baby. I said to Jake, 'I'm just not enjoying this. I'm sorry to moan, but this place doesn't even have the basic things.'

He agreed and said, 'Let's look for somewhere else tomorrow.'

If it had been a holiday where I could get drunk, I wouldn't have cared. If I hadn't been pregnant, I'd just have got pissed out of my head and dealt with it. But I just wanted some nice comforts and to be happy.

To be honest, I think if they'd have found a way to make me a strawberry milkshake I'd have stayed! I went to a restaurant in Newcastle once and when I asked for one, they said they didn't sell milkshakes at all, but then ten minutes later they came over to me and they'd made one from scratch. If they can do it in a bar, they can do it in a hotel!

We sat all night looking on the hotels.com website. We eventually found an amazing hotel nearby – but it was bloody expensive. We knew it was going to cost us an arm and a leg. But I would have given away both arms, legs and my whole head at that stage! We needed to let the hotel know, but I wanted to avoid the awkward situation – so Jake had to tell them (I told you he is the best boyfriend ever).

When we got to the next place it was BEYOND AMAZING. As soon as we arrived, we instantly relaxed. It was incredible. We were so chilled and happy and cocooned in our love bubble.

The baby shower . . . that turned into an actual shower . . . of rain

I decided to have the baby shower at my house and obviously I didn't let anyone else do any of the planning because I'm a stupid control freak. I *had* to do everything myself. And clearly it wasn't ever going to be just a normal baby shower – it had to have at least five levels to the day. Why on earth I wanted to plan something that complicated and confusing is beyond me.

For forty-five days before the date, I watched the weather forecast, like I was literally THE WEATHER GIRL. And only on the day before the event did the weather decide to change to rain. Well, it was all planned to be outside and I had no cover and no time to sort anything either. So, I just had to hope for the best. The day started and it was all sunny and bright and I said to me mam, 'We've done it. It's going to be like this all day. I've cheated the gods!'

The day started at 3pm, with everyone arriving and mingling and a bartender team called Hey, Bartender putting on a show and playing fun drinking games with the guests. When people were coming in, they were all being treated so well. Then at 3.30pm we had canapés and bread and cheese going round. Then 4pm was when everyone sat down for the starters and mains. It was all going smoothly – so far so good. The sun was coming out but then it was going in again, then at one point it started to spit a little bit, but no one was really bothered because it was so minor. People were all at the table, having a great time and a laugh. Then, as soon as everyone's main courses came out on the tables, the heavens opened, and it poured. Not just any ordinary rain – this was THE HEAVIEST, WETTEST RAIN YOU HAVE EVER SEEN. You can't even imagine the downpour. Everyone had napkins over their heads. All the food was getting soaking wet. And I am stressing, 'Oh my God! What do I do in this situation?' I'd planned the whole day to be in the garden! All of the games were planned around the area where we were sitting for the meal – there was even an assault course and all sorts. I had gone to town! I was looking round at all my friends and family and the rain was pouring down and everyone was running away from the table to hide in the pool room. Someone said to me, 'Charlotte, you're not stressed, are you? We're having a great time?' I was thinking, 'I AM MORE STRESSED THAN I HAVE EVER BEEN IN MY LIFE!' because I had a big surprise planned for the end of the night. And it was all meant to happen outside – we'd had rehearsals and everything. I was thinking, 'How the hell am I going to make this work inside?' There were about thirty people there in total, plus the film crew from *Charlotte in Sunderland* and also a team from a magazine who had arranged to cover it. So, it's fair to say, there was A LOT going on.

I didn't know where to put myself. I wanted to hide in a corner. In the end I dragged everyone inside. I had people crammed on the sofa in front of the TV with their main courses on their laps. Some of them were squashed round the dining-room table. There were a few people at the breakfast bar and people at the bar stools and in the cinema room. I was looking around and thinking, 'How the hell am I going to rearrange everything now?'

We still got to play some of the games I'd planned, but only the ones we could do inside, the ones that were a bit simpler. So we did Stick the Sperm on Jake's Balls, which was a really funny one, and then we had Diaper Pong, which was like beer pong, but you had to fling the balls and try to get them in the nappies. We had the downing of the drink in the baby bottles to see who could down the drink fastest.

Then, after that, it was time for the BIG SURPRISE – a Beyoncé brunch with three drag queens! We'd planned and rehearsed that they would burst into the garden when we were outside and do a big performance in the big space around the tables. We'd even made an elevated stage for them to stand on. But now we'd had to bring the tables in from the outside and make up some more tables so that everyone was sitting in a good order, so we were all just crammed in the house. The drag queens were all waiting in a hotel up the road so I had to try and sneakily video where they would need to come inside and what the new set-up was and send it to them.

The door opened and the first queen, Cara Melle, came in. But the song was wrong and we had to reset it so everyone saw her! The surprise was RUINED! I was slumped in a corner behind the DJ booth, and I honestly just slid down the wall thinking, 'I can't take much more of this. It has been one disaster after another.' It just wasn't ending and the film crew were getting it all on camera. I just sat there with my head in my hands saying, 'I just want this all to be over! I don't know why I ever decided to make it all so complicated.'

I shouldn't really have worried. When the queens all came out and did their performances everyone was having the

162

best time. People were standing on the dining-room table, everyone was going wild. But my God I was so stressed.

With only a few weeks to my due date, stress levels were going to be sent up a few more notches after that – because not only did we have the nursery still to finish, but Jake and I had to pack our bags and get ready for a little vacation in London. We were moving to a rental flat to be near the hospital in the last weeks of my pregnancy . . . the clock was ticking for the big birth-day!

My Birthing Playlist

Given how I like to plan everything to be absolutely perfect, a birthing playlist was a MUST. So Jake and I spent hours prepping this wonderful list of music for when our little girl first entered the world. Now, some people might be surprised to hear that my taste in music is a bit on the depressing side. Whenever I go to karaoke and sing a song people end up crying in a corner because it's all so morbid.

This was the original list I had planned for and my reasons for the songs:

Billie Eilish, 'Ocean Eyes'
This is my ultimate fave! I love all her music but this one seems the most calming one to start with.

Coldplay, 'Yellow'
I love Coldplay soooo much. Me and my mam just went to see them – it was on our bucket list. It was such a special night to us and when this one came on it was amazing.

Norah Jones, 'Come Away With Me'
This is the playlist of my childhood! My mam's fave and in turn mine. I love all her songs but this one is beautiful and so soothing and calming.

Damien Rice, 'The Blower's Daughter'

This is just another calm one. And to be perfectly honest I'm starting to run out of ideas.

Joji, 'Glimpse of Us'

I heard this as a trending sound on Instagram and it's absolutely beautiful! Makes me cry just hearing it.

Oasis, 'Half the World Away'

This is Jake's favourite song. The doctor thinks she will be out by this track, *maybe* Jake will be holding her and that will be such a lovely memory for him.

Ed Sheeran, 'Give me Love'

This is another Jake choice. Better not hog the whole playlist to myself.

David Gray, 'Babylon'

No reason in the slightest but I'm totally out of ideas and I just enjoy the song.

Jamiroquai, 'Cosmic Girl'

Because she's going to be a little cosmic girl. Hahahahhaha. I love this song and want to end on a lovely high!

A day before we were due to go into the hospital, Jake and I then had a mad panic that we had too many slow sad songs on the list so we revisited it all and did a new playlist removing ones like Damien Rice and replacing them with Beyoncé and Ariana Grande for some more upbeat vibes!

11

My baby is . . .

giving me rollercoaster hormones!

It's 2am and something's awoken me,
I struggle to get up,
THIS BUMP IS HEAVY,
It's dark and it's scary,
I can't even SEE!
What could be going on?
Oh yeah – I just need another FUCKING WEE!
I'm sick in the morning,
I'm sick in the night,
I'm sick when I'm sleeping,
It gives me a fright,
When riding in the car . . . guess what?
I'm sick there,
Sometimes I'm left finding,
Lumps of sick in my hair.

In the last few weeks of my pregnancy, even though I still had a lot of aches and pains, I finally felt like I could enjoy it and get properly excited. I didn't feel so much of a zombie any more and I got my personality back a bit. Also just being able to feel the baby kicking was amazing. It was so cute knowing she was there, wriggling about inside me. I actually did love the bump too. After I had Alba, I kind of missed it. It was such a comfort thing being able to stroke it and hold it.

Isn't it just so amazing how your body changes? I'm in awe of it all.

All the stuff your body goes through is crazy. But the hormones . . . my Lord! I never knew it was possible to get so emotional – I lost count of how many times I just cried and cried when I was pregnant. Literally I just started crying at anything.

At last I had stopped being sick. My morning sickness started at about six weeks, and it was HORRENDOUS. It hit me so bad. I was puking about five times a day. I don't know why they call it morning sickness – because it was morning, noon, afternoon, night, dusk . . .! There might have been a day when I was only sick once – now that was a lucky day. I never had a break! I can only describe the feeling as like food poisoning – constant food poisoning every single day! I was just constantly feeling sick. Every car journey I'd have to take a bag with me in case I vommed. I discovered that ginger is really good for sickness – those little shots you can get in the shops were brilliant so I took them all off the shelves. During those first weeks I felt bad for feeling so ill and exhausted and tired and faint because I thought, 'I need to be grateful I'm pregnant!'

I desperately wanted to have a craving at the start because people kept asking me if I had any. One day I was in the car with Jake and I drank this Lipton Ice Tea and I said to him, 'Oh yum, this might just be my craving.' About two days later, the doorbell rang and it was a crate of Lipton Ice Tea that Jake had ordered for me! I still have about sixty bottles and I never want to see one ever again. But as time went on, I developed a few real cravings:

1. Mr Freeze ice pops – or just any kind of ice.
2. Pickled Onion Space Invader crisps – also a big MUST – the big super bags though, not the piddly little ones.
3. ANY kind of chocolate – but most of all Minstrels and Mars Bar cakes (which aren't actually a type of cake at all, they're just Rice Krispies with a Mars melted on top).
4. Blackcurrant Ribena Light – one of my absolute deepest cravings of the whole lot. It was so heavenly that I drank it morning, night, afternoon, dusk and dawn. I needed to check into some kind of Ribena rehab afterwards!

People say your sense of smell is so intense when you're pregnant too. Before I got pregnant I used to LOVE Jake's aftershave, but all of a sudden when he came over and hugged me when he was wearing it I would start retching! I used to love green olives too but I couldn't bear the sight of them.

What happened to happy hormones?

When I was around eight or nine weeks pregnant, suddenly, out of nowhere, I took a dive. I felt so low, so down, there was this dark cloud over me. I had zero energy – I was so tired I couldn't get off the sofa or speak to anyone. But I was too embarrassed to say I was feeling down. I kept thinking, 'This is meant to be the happiest time of my life – what the hell is wrong with me?' The first day I started feeling like it, Jake was trying to talk to me, and I was huffing and puffing. I was thinking, 'Why am I being such a bitch?' I would barely speak to him. He told me he remembers that day – he made himself busy and got out of the house because I looked like I didn't want him to be there with me. He didn't want to sit there awkwardly.

But I had crashed into such a slump, and I couldn't understand what was wrong. I didn't feel myself and started panicking that I was going to feel like this for my whole pregnancy. I felt horrendous, I felt listless, I felt sad, I couldn't stop crying. I had never felt anything like it. It can only be described as a depressed feeling. I would wake up in the morning and I did

170

not have an ounce of enthusiasm to want to get out of bed. I got really scared. I'd never seen anyone else talk about it before and I didn't know who to turn to. It had just hit me out of the blue. I thought, 'Oh my God, why am I feeling like this? What do I do?' But I didn't want to make a scene. The very last thing you want when you're pregnant is to seem sad, because you should be happy. And I wasn't properly sad. I was happy I was pregnant, but I was feeling sad inside. I did know that hormones can do mad stuff to you in pregnancy, it's very common. But this wasn't just me being moody. This was a different feeling altogether. I didn't even want to get out of bed. I was having dark feelings and I never had any dark feelings usually. I couldn't move and there was a cloud over my head. I didn't want to tell anyone because I didn't want to seem ungrateful. So I kept it inside and then it obviously just built up and got worse. Each day I would wake up and the feeling still hadn't shifted. There was a constant darkness over everything, and I couldn't even be bothered trying to have a conversation. Any time Jake spoke to me, I'd just give him one-word answers. I literally couldn't even string a sentence together.

I didn't know how to explain how I was feeling either. I hadn't told anyone I was pregnant, which made it even more difficult. I was so worried that I started googling it and ended up on these forums in the middle of the night – under an alias name – asking people what the symptoms could mean. Because I couldn't speak to anyone I knew about it, I was asking strangers – but no one replied! I was typing questions like, 'Hi there, I'm nine weeks pregnant and I'm feeling really low and depressed. Is this normal? Will it go away?' I can't remember what my alias was – I think it was a load of numbers.

I would check the forums every day. There was never one response. But there were so many other women writing that they felt the same way! People were saying they were feeling depressed in the first trimester. One of them wrote, 'We've been trying for a baby for four years and I should be the happiest I've ever been. But why am I feeling like so depressed and sad?' So I started thinking that this must be a little more normal than I thought, and that helped me a little bit. But no one was leaving a real name – it was like none of us wanted to show our real selves because we all felt so bad that we felt this way. I just wanted someone to speak to about it, someone who felt the same way, to make me feel like I wasn't just going crazy. I kept trying to reach out so someone would write back to me – but no one ever did.

I didn't dare ask my doctor because I felt like I was being stupid and that he might think it was a trivial problem. I didn't want to bother him. I just kind of stuck it out. Thankfully I didn't feel suicidal or anything like that. I know some people do feel that way or feel that they don't even want the baby. That never once crossed my mind, thank God. I just felt like there was nothing to be excited about. I've spoken to other people since and loads of them have told me they felt the same way. There's just never anyone who talks about it openly – and there should be. Hopefully even me saying this now will help some people know they're not going crazy.

After a bit of research, I found out that it could be something called pre-natal depression. Wow, that sounded scary. It sent me into even more of a mad panic. I got this app which helps you keep a track of your mood when you're pregnant. I decided I needed to keep a diary of it and log how I was feeling. I couldn't fathom whether I had felt this bad three days ago or not so I needed to get some sort of control.

Jake didn't know what was going on with me – he was really concerned. I didn't say anything to him for a while because I felt embarrassed and I didn't want him to worry. In the end I had to say something because I was crying my eyes out so much, there was no hiding it. Once I finally opened up to him, just the act of speaking it out loud, getting it out of my mouth, made me feel so much better. I said, 'I just feel really low. I don't know why and I can't tell you why, but this is how I'm feeling.' He was relieved to be honest, because I had been so off with him! I didn't want him thinking that I was starting to have second thoughts about the baby – he's a worrier like that. But it was good that I'd finally expressed myself. He was really understanding, and it was a weight off my shoulders.

I am so glad I spoke about it in the end as it just made me feel so less alone. After that whenever I told Jake I was feeling something or having any symptoms, he just researched it straight away. He was so amazing throughout the pregnancy, constantly trying to find solutions to what I was going through.

It must have been about ten days before the cloud eventually lifted and I started to feel normal again. I think it was just this massive hormone imbalance. But I was really scared that it was going to come back when I gave birth and my hormones went through another big change and that it might last even longer. I wasn't sure if I would be able to cope with that. I didn't really know what I would do.

I think it's so important that people open up about this stuff though. The best thing I learnt through that whole time was to talk about it. When you are thinking things on your own it can really spiral and make you so much worse. You are your own worst enemy and you overthink and get into a right pickle in your mind. If you are ever feeling low when you're pregnant, you must never beat yourself up about it. Hormones are very powerful things that mess with your mind! But it all balances out in the end. Now I know that a lot of women feel like this and I feel really strongly that people need to know it's OK to open up. So my advice is – talk to someone! I wouldn't want to go back to that feeling. I really wouldn't. And remember it isn't going to last forever.

Chemo, chemo, chemo chameleon

My hormones were up and down through my whole pregnancy and Mam's cancer just made everything even more exaggerated. It was both a relief and a panic when she eventually had the surgery a few weeks before the baby was due to remove the tumour and reconstruct her breast at the same time. She ended up in surgery for five and half hours and it felt like three months. The wait was horrible. But the result was better than we could have ever dreamed. They removed the tumour, the diseased tissue and three lymph nodes. Cancer hadn't spread to her lymph nodes and the tumour was smaller than they thought, it was 11 millimetres, not 19 millimetres like they had first told us. Apparently to cut open the boob and then reconstruct it takes a longer time than it takes to completely lose your breast. They cut her from the side and took skin from underneath her arm to build it again. They took 12 centimetres out of Mam – that is a big chunk of boob. But the results were incredible. I said, 'Mam, it's like you've had a mini boob job.'

Even though we were told she was basically cancer-free, the doctors also warned us that because the type of cancer she'd had was such an aggressive, fast-spreading one, they wanted to be sure to zap it completely. So the doctor suggested she had a course of chemo and then five days of back-to-back radiotherapy, to make sure all the cells in her body were blasted and prevent the cancer coming back. She was scared because she knew this was a big deal and not an easy treatment to go through – but there's no way we'd have let her say no to having it. We didn't want to go through this again so would do anything to prevent it returning.

She started the chemo with a big brave smile on her face, knowing it was for the best. I was determined to support her through every step of her journey. We knew it would be intense, but I was determined to be with her as much as possible. I just hated the fact that I was getting so heavily pregnant because I felt that the focus and attention should all be on her.

I didn't want to leave Mam's side during her treatments, and I wanted to make her feel as special and looked after as possible. The first time we arrived at the hospital she sat in the chair and just started crying. It was really daunting. I guess walking into that ward and being faced with it head on must have really hit her. My eyes were filling up with tears, so I kept turning to the side to stop her from seeing me. I was thinking, 'God, this is so hard – but I can't cry!' So, I held her hand and told her it was going to be tough but we would get through it together.

The chemo sessions knocked her for six a little bit. She was always left feeling so wiped out and tired. She had it on a Tuesday, then on Wednesday she usually felt fine, but Thursday and Friday were really bad days (I realise that sounds a bit like I'm singing a Craig David song about the cancer ward . . .). I went with her for the first couple and to keep her mind off stuff, because she was in there for hours, we played cards (I call it 'Threes' but some people call it 'Shithead' it's so fun and a great way to pass the time). We also took the piss out of each other and the mad goings on around the ward. We were always laughing and I knew exactly how to distract her. I just wish this hadn't all happened when I was so heavily pregnant as it meant I couldn't do as much for her as I wanted to.

Mam was also sad about the prospect of losing her hair from the chemo. It's not something you can predict though – you can't say a definitive yes or no. Some people don't lose theirs at all. I didn't want her to feel embarrassed or self-conscious about anything, or that she had anything to hide. I wanted to make sure she felt as good as possible, so we found an amazing wig shop in London. The cost of a decent wig is like the cost of a deposit for a car – but I told her she was worth every penny because I wanted her to feel in a better place.

We made a real day of it and had such a laugh trying loads of different hair-dos. I tried some of the wigs on and quickly realised I definitely don't suit having a fringe! There was another wig I forced her to try and it was dead long and blond. I've honestly never seen her looking so damn GLAM-OROUS! She loved it but she didn't feel as comfortable as with the other one – and they're not cheap so we couldn't get two. Eventually she found one she fell in love with – long and brunette – and she didn't want to leave without it.

She needn't have worried so much in the end as she didn't lose as much hair as she thought. She wore a cold cap during the treatments, which really helps some people. It worked for Mam and she was over the moon. She still wore the wig sometimes though because she couldn't have extensions when she was wearing the cap. And she loves an extension does me mam!

Mam's cancer made her really conscious about the fact that you don't start having regular mammograms until you are fifty. She met one girl at the hospital who had the same cancer as her, oestrogen positive, and she was only twenty-seven years old. She was a nurse working on a cancer ward and she found a lump in her breast. Her doctor thought it was nothing but referred her and it turned out it was cancer. Mam did an interview with a newspaper to talk about what she was going through and to try to raise awareness; she wanted to use her spotlight for some good. She said she wanted to encourage older women to go to their mammogram appointments and younger women to check their breasts regularly and be conscious of their boob health.

All of this made me become so much more aware of my own body too. I found a lump literally just after Mam was diagnosed. I went to get it checked out straight away. Luckily it was nothing bad – but can you even imagine?! The anniversary of Sarah Harding's death from breast cancer in September really hit me and me mam hard. Sarah hadn't really spoken about it in public much before she died and it seemed like it all happened so quickly after that; all of a sudden, she was gone. It was so heart-breaking hearing the rest of Girls Aloud paying tribute to her a year later, and I know Mam couldn't stop thinking about it. It was smack in the middle of when she was having her chemo and just the mention of it on the news kept sending her back into her dark place.

Thank God for the men in our lives like Dad and Jake. I think Dad has found Mam's cancer incredibly hard to deal with, but he holds it all in and keeps it together for the sake of the family. He's been so solid and calm and by her side like glue the whole time. She's his rock too and for her to be so poorly must have been so tough for him, but he's never been able to show it. Having someone in your family with cancer just does all kinds of weird stuff to your emotions and it really makes you value every single life moment and cherish all the times you have together.

Halfway through September me and Jake moved temporarily down to London to be near the hospital. Although we weren't in the comfort of home and it was hard to be so far away from Mam, it was actually a nice time for us to be alone and get used to what was about to happen and how our LIVES WERE ABOUT TO TOTALLY CHANGE.

Just as we were coming down to stay in London, the Queen died! Wasn't that such a sad, pivotal moment in time? Jake and I were just staring at the TV the whole time thinking how weird it was that our baby would never know this amazing queen, this brilliant female ruler, and our longest reigning monarch. Jake and I both cried watching the funeral. I mean, we cry at most things anyway, we cry all the time, but this was really something. We cried, cried, cried watching the processions and seeing the family and their faces. We were sobbing our eyes out all that day!

By now I was getting absolutely massive but the sickness was subsiding, thank God. I was hardly sleeping – I couldn't get to sleep until about 2am. (I think maybe it's because your body is preparing you for the lack of sleep you're going to get when the baby arrives.) Jake was doing so much for me – literally waiting on me hand and foot because I was finding it so hard to move about and everything was aching like mad. I could hardly stand up and spent most of the few days leading up to the birth lying horizontally on the sofa, eating orange ice pops. He was cooking for me and picking up all my clothes after me – everything. I looked at him one day and thought, he must be so sick of this! I felt so useless and I just lay in bed and cried my eyes out. Then when I was crying I was feeling even worse, but I couldn't stop. I was inconsolable. As you know, I was crying over anything and everything. Sometimes I didn't even know what I was crying about – it might have been that I forgot to put the bins out or just that Jake was at work and I missed him.

I just could not wait until I had my little girl in my arms. Every time I thought about it, I cried. One minute I'd be scared, then excited, then scared again. Then I'd be in tears in a mad panic in case I tried to burp her and no burp came out . . .??? In those last few days I was just overcome with this rollercoaster of emotions.

Some of the Things I've Cried Over Because of the Hormones

1. Forgetting to put the bins out.

2. Walking up the stairs and picturing a baby crawling around in the house.

3. Jake bringing home some comfy clothes for me to wear because I said nothing fitted.

4. Jake saying he had to go to work and me feeling sad because I'd miss him.

5. When we were filming against the green screen for *Geordie Shore* (this is the bit where you're talking to camera about different things that have happened) and the producer started asking me about Jake. I got so hysterical I couldn't speak – I was so emotional talking about him and the fact that I loved him so much, that they had to call the whole thing off and send the camera crew home! I was such a mess, it was literally as if someone had just died in front of me!

6. Watching *Jurassic Park* because Jake had never seen it before and seeing it all again through fresh eyes reminded me how good it was. This was, after all, my original life inspiration and the reason for wanting to be an archaeologist (or should that have been a palaeontologist?).

7. People saying how happy they were for me that I'd fallen pregnant.

8. Jake and Nathaniel bonding.

9. Feeling useless because Jake was doing everything for me. I have got no words for where I would be in my life if Jake didn't exist. He was literally washing up, cleaning, wiping the benches, doing everything around the kitchen, putting all the dishes in the dishwasher.

10. Jake teaching himself to cook steak from YouTube for me! He never used to know how to cook before! And he put it with all the sauces we both like – Béarnaise, peppercorn, Diane, mushroom. How amazing is that! But it just made me cry more because I didn't do anything. All I would do was get out of bed, sit down somewhere, then go back to bed again. I was like a big lump doing nothing! I was sobbing my eyes out thinking, 'How will I ever repay him? He's not going to want to be with me! What if he dumps me?!!'

12

My baby is . . .

keeping me awake at night with worry

Having a baby is an actual massive bloody JOB isn't it? Why don't people have BEING A PARENT as the main achievement on their CVs, because I can't think of any career that's bigger or more fulfilling.

Towards the end of my pregnancy, I would look at myself in the mirror before I went to bed and think, 'Having a baby is a scary, scary thought!' It felt so weird knowing there was a HUMAN GROWING INSIDE OF ME. One night I started thinking too much about it and made myself scared thinking it was like *Alien: Resurrection*. I am amazed by what women's bodies can do but it also freaked me out a bit.

I know there are some people who would say, 'I'm so ready!' but I couldn't say that because I was absolutely shitting myself. It's such a big life change – was I ready for that life change? For thirty-two years of my life I'd had no huge responsibilities and literally done whatever the hell I wanted. And that was all about to change. I was scared about everything – whether I'd bond with the baby, whether I was going to be a good parent, or if I'd know what I was doing. My mind was whirring and wondering what the birth was going to be like and if anything was going to go wrong. Then the next minute, I'd start panicking about the fear of post-natal depression as I know it can affect some women and it's awful. Because I'd had that moment during my pregnancy when I felt so, so incredibly low and I just couldn't control it I was panicking that it was going to happen again. But I had so much support I knew deep down I didn't need to be in such a flap.

A lot of that support was from people on Instagram. I know some people get really angry when other people start telling you what to do when it comes to motherhood. But I actually loved it! Even if someone sent me a message that seemed a bit pushy, or a little bit rude at first, I just thought, 'Keep them coming!' Because, honestly, in all of those messages there would be about five or six where I'd learn something really important. And I love the fact that I have a community of fans – thousands of people I don't even know – who are there trying to help me.

Jake was slightly scared as well. Maybe a bit less than me, but he was still shitting it. We'd only been together a year – and we realised he had known me longer pregnant than not pregnant! I'd only been not pregnant for four months of us knowing each other. We'd had more sober pregnant times than we'd had honeymoon fun times. He was so excited at the same time. He kept saying he couldn't wait to be a dad.

Me mam and dad were beyond themselves with excitement about being grandparents – they bought a cot and loads of baby stuff for their house. But I think the best thing for them was the fact that they knew they would be able to give the baby back when they'd had enough!

I had a long hard think about how much I was going to post about the baby on social media. I'm a bit of a control freak and even though I would usually do a magazine shoot I knew Jake would hate it. It makes him feel incredibly uncomfortable, so to be in the magazine with loads of strangers on set watching him would have been too much. He absolutely hates being in front of the camera, he's not like that at all. But I do get it, it is a daunting thing, standing in a room trying to pose with everyone looking at you. You can feel so awkward. So I knew that would be a bit of a problem.

I was also worried about all the emotions I would go through. Then I started thinking about what people might say about the baby if I posted a picture on social media. What if a troll decided to say the baby looked like a potato? Can you imagine how I'd feel then, as a new mother with hormones raging all over the place? I don't think that would go down well! And then I might want to try to track that troll down. I could get arrested and imprisoned because you can say what you want about me but my child is a whole different kettle of fish!

In the end, I knew I did want to share the special moment, but I wanted to share it in a controlled way. So I created a newsletter called *Charlotte's First Look*, which allowed me to send emails and some personal pictures to people who signed up. There was a lovely little community on there where we could all chat – a nice safe space away from the trolls!

I was obviously always going to put my little girl on Instagram eventually, it was just the beginning of the parent journey I was nervous about. Probably by the time you read this I will have made loads of TikTok videos with her doing dance routines. But for the first few months, I just wanted to be in my little baby bubble where nothing was too out there or exposed.

Sleep training – surely four legs are the same as two?

I have a confession – I didn't read one book. I didn't have a clue about burping the baby or any of that stuff. All my friends who had babies bought all these books and manuals and spent hours doing crazy things like birthing plans. When we found out we were going to have to stay in London in the flat for a few days after the birth, Mam brought us a baby bath, I didn't even know how to bath a baby and I had to google it! So, the first thing I ever researched was 'baby bathing' on YouTube. I watched a tutorial and got in a panic that I wouldn't be able to do it.

But when it came to looking after a newborn baby – I figured there must be no better way to prepare than by bringing up . . . dogs. And let's face it, I have loads of them. Only problem is – none of them are sleep trained and they all just do what they want.

It was about eight weeks before the baby was due, and I suddenly realised we were going to have to do something about the dogs being in our bed all the time. The baby was going to have to sleep in a cot in our room and some-times would be in our bed – and currently my dogs think that's their space and their sanctuary. I had visions of them crawling all over my poor child and squashing her or farting on her head in the night.

So we decided it was time to sleep train the dogs.

Jake's never had dogs before so he's not as soppy or obsessed with them as I am. He doesn't have that same rush of love towards an animal – and especially not mine, because mine are a bit annoying. So at first, when we met, it was really weird for him to come into my house with dogs all sleeping wherever they want. Rhubarb sleeps on the floor, but Baby and Banana are on the bed. Banana's like an actual baby. He's up and down all night – I was getting up about four times in the night with him to let him outside for a wee.

One of Jake's businesses is a chauffeur company, and some

of his clients are footballers who he has to drive round Manchester. He has a contract with Man City and he loves football so he will never give up that Man City contract. But this means that for most of his jobs he has to get up really early in the morning. He's a grafter and doesn't care about the fact he's so far away. He will just do it. But when he was first at mine he got really agitated with the dogs. And he gets frightened easily too. Banana will growl at you if you touch him in the bed so Jake would roll over and Banana would go mad! His sleep got so disturbed by the dogs that at one point I ended up having to sleep in the other room with them so they didn't keep waking him up. It was honestly like having a baby.

But I knew I had to take action before we had a real baby. So, I set up a room downstairs in the house and made it literally the cosiest den you can ever imagine. I made it the most perfect dog heaven with a dog crate, dog beds and blankets. Then I got a camera installed and put a baby gate on the door. I had it all figured out. I was going to use that room whenever I left the house so they knew it was their safe place and their little room. And then we started sleep training them to sleep in their den downstairs. I knew it would be hard but I had to brace myself for it.

The first night I did it, I was staring at the camera obsessively all night and didn't sleep a wink. I was watching them! I was like a detective with my notebook, writing down all the details of when they barked and what time they stopped. This way, I figured, every night I could see if there was any progression. Baby and Rhubarb were not the problem – it was Banana. Baby and Rhubarb had a little bark then slept fine all night and that was the same every single day really. But Banana barked ALL NIGHT LONG on the first night. By the end of the second night he'd been barking slightly less and less. There was a lot of progress. He went from barking all night to barking for a while, stopping for a bit and then going again. After seven nights I felt that we'd almost cracked it.

But then Jake and I had to move down to London and I had to leave the dogs with me mam and dad at their house, so it was like starting all over again! And poor Mam had a nightmare. The problem is, we've spoilt them! They've been in the family for seven years and we treat them like royalty. We literally cook them scrambled eggs and ham and shower them with cuddles and love, they couldn't be more spoiled if they tried. We love them so much. But that first two days of doing sleep training, I have to admit I was lying in bed thinking, 'Should I get rid of Banana?'

Dad, who is obsessed with Banana, wouldn't ever have a bad word said about him. But once he was in their care and me and Jake were in the flat in London, even he was saying, 'Right – where can we send him?!' Banana was being an absolute nightmare and barking all night long again. But it's our own fault, as we shouldn't have spoiled him this much. The other two weren't a problem – they slept fine at Mam and Dad's. It's Banana, he thinks he's human. At both houses we'd given him the snuggest little room downstairs, swaddled with blankets and cushions, water bowls, food and toys. But we needed to just be strong and persevere. I looked online and saw that some people say it can take two weeks to a month to do the training properly.

What made it worse was that Mam was going through chemotherapy while she had them with her. So I was frantically researching everything, thinking I need to try and find a solution to help speed things up. The daytime wasn't a problem, but they can't be constantly doing training techniques with the dog through the night. Poor Mam needs to rest and Dad has work so he can't be up all night either. One of me mates said they used a spray bottle with water – they said just give Banana a squirt in the face if he's playing up. So that worked for a bit.

In the end I found something called a dog training collar, which said it was one of the most humane ways to train. If the dog starts barking for a long time it just lets off a high-pitched sound and gives a vibration and that stops them – no electric shock, no pain, nothing like that. And it had four hundred 4-star reviews online – all of them from people in the dog community who said it was brilliant. So we all decided we'd try it for a week.

When it arrived, Dad tweeted a picture of it saying, 'This collar is going on tonight. Let's see how it goes.' And then he got loads of trolls and animal-rights activists bombarding him on Twitter saying he was being cruel and unfair and unjust. I went mad. People were going on and on at us. There was one woman called Mandy who was so annoying, she wouldn't leave Dad alone and I was so angry with her. I said, 'Mandy – Fuck off! There's nothing cruel about it. It's tiny and it's got a sound and vibration feature which only goes on at night time.'

It worked though! When Banana barked in the night it went off once and he must have felt the vibration and heard the sound and thought, 'Oh, I don't like that.' Never barked again that night. So we only needed to keep it on him for a couple more nights and then slowly took it off. He was quiet again for that third night, then started a tiny bit again on the fourth so we had to put it back on him for a couple more nights. But then it was completely off and Mam, Dad and Nathaniel could sleep – all was right in the world!

That Twitter tirade just made me think how hard it was going to be when I had the baby and if I put anything up about the fact that I wasn't breastfeeding or anything to do with sleep training. Everyone would have some sort of opinion and it was going to make me want to set everyone's houses on fire!

To push or not to push

One thing I was a bit worried about talking about publicly was the fact that I had decided to have a C-section. I was so scared that people would criticise me and say I was cheating or something. But when I sat down with Mr Okaro at around twelve weeks, when we knew we still had a heartbeat and everything was fine, he'd asked, 'What do you want to do about the birth?' I told him that (a) I was a bit frightened, partly because having been in the hospital and been through the trauma of the ectopic I felt like I might have a panic attack and a flashback being in there again and feeling out of control. And also (b) that every single one of my friends had had some kind of horror-story – none of them seemed to emerge with a great report from trying a natural birth!

He said, 'Listen, I'm an obstetrician. This is my job. And after all you went through with the ectopic, I think you should get a C-section.' I've heard friends say that their own doctors have told them, 'Don't believe anyone who says that everything's fine and goes back to normal afterwards. You can tear and rip and some of it can be irreversible. There are now so many more advanced ways to bring a baby into the world.'

Some people have amazing natural births and swear by them but equally I know others who have had bad experiences. If it goes wrong, it can do your body irreversible damage. Every single one of my friends who had had kids had told me something that freaked me out about the birth. Honestly, I had not heard one nice tale! So I didn't think the odds were really in favour of me having the most perfect birth. I don't have the luckiest track record!

One of my best friends, Christina, whom I've been mates

with for twelve years, had a really traumatic first birth and said 'never again'. But Marnie's story was the one that stuck with me the most. She suffered the most agonising pain and knew something terrible was happening to her body. She ended up with an irreversible bladder condition and had to have a blood transfusion because she lost so much blood. She also caught a rare bacterial infection while giving birth, was bed-bound for weeks and couldn't bond with her baby. That was enough to freak me out for life. Then, for the first two years of Rox's life, she said she was the most depressed she's ever been. She'd felt so guilty because she couldn't give him the love and attention he needed because she was so low, she was ill and she was still in so much pain. Marnie had a planned C-section for her second baby and told me, 'Charlotte – I cannot believe the difference in how it went.' But this time around she said it was so completely different. Everyone expects you to be the most perfect mother and you sometimes can't be.

I was all over the place for ages feeling like I *should* choose a natural birth while not really wanting to. I remember when we were on holiday in Mauritius and we got chatting to a South African couple around the pool who had five kids. They'd obviously noticed that I was pregnant (it was pretty difficult not to, seeing as I looked like a giant dinosaur egg) and the woman was asking me lots of questions about the birth. 'Are you going to have a natural one or a C-section?'

I said to her, 'If I'm honest the reason I've been so reluctant to say anything is because in England if you were to openly say you want a C-section, there's so much stigma around it. It's like it's really quite frowned upon.' I told her I felt pressured to go for a natural labour, because then I would be able to say I'd done it and everyone could be dead proud of me.

'Wait, hold on!' she said, looking all concerned. 'That is not the mentality that you should have when giving birth! You shouldn't be thinking you have to have a natural labour so that everyone around you approves! You need to get that out of your head!' Then she told me, 'We had every single child as a C-section.'

I looked shocked. 'Really? Was that your choice? What was the reason behind that?'

She told me that in South Africa everyone who has private health care tends to opt for a C-section, because they believe it is the safest way to bring a child into the world.

In the end I thought, 'God forbid if anything was to happen or if I was to get poorly. I would never forgive myself that I had had a natural birth just to please everyone else.' Given the flashbacks I still had due to the trauma of the ectopic pregnancy, I felt confident that a C-section was the right choice for me. The thought of it was still scary, because I knew I was going to be sliced open through loads of layers of skin and muscle but, ultimately, I made the decision that was best for me and the baby. I wanted to keep my mind and my fanny in the best condition possible! Also this way we could properly plan it. So, when we got back from

Mauritius, we booked the date for the birth there and then – 14th October 2022. How mad and crazy to know the actual day you are going to go into hospital and have your child! BEST PRESENT EVER!

Once we had the date booked it was time to start planning for the big day. There are so many different opinions on what to take, what to prepare and what to do. I had so much advice on what things my head nearly exploded!

Although I had the date booked in for 14th October, I packed my bag about a month beforehand JUST IN CASE OF EMERGENCIES. Here's what I packed:

1. Three long t-shirts – I'm unsure why I thought I needed them, but hey.
2. Wool socks! – I somehow managed to get athlete's foot, which was very depressing as I used to think I had nice feet. Apparently it's a thing some people get in the third trimester – it's very rare so OBVIOUSLY I WAS GOING TO GET IT! I had to sit with my feet in apple cider vinegar to get rid of it.
3. Bridget Jones knickers – no point trying to be sexy when your insides have just been pulled out.
4. Tight bra – this was an important one for me because I didn't want to breastfeed. So I had to have a tight bra that put pressure on my boobs. They would still produce milk but the more they were fixed the less they would be stimulated and keep leaking.

5. Nipple pads – even with tight t-shirts I was told there would be leakage. They're like panty pads but for your boobs!

When I announced on Instagram I was having a C-section I was scared about all the negativity that was going to come – that everyone would be saying I should be doing what nature intended and telling me I was too posh too push. But I needn't have been so worried as I didn't have any of that. Everyone was so positive and supportive about it. I think in the end, people knew how hard it had been for me because of the ectopic and understood it was my doctor's advice.

13

My baby is . . .

the size of a melon and she's on her way OUT

Two nights before I was due to go into hospital, Jake and I went to the pub for our last date before becoming Mam and Dad.

And we cried our eyes out for hours.

We sat opposite each other and were literally staring into each other's eyes across the table with tears streaming down our faces. We'd been rushing about so much in the last few days that this was the first proper moment we could take it all in. And the whole thing just hit us so hard, but in wonderful ways. We were completely and utterly overwhelmed with emotion. We sat there frozen in time and Jake said to me, 'This is going to be the biggest thing that happens to either of us. This is the most amazing thing we will probably do in our entire lives.' At that exact moment, I got a message on my phone from a friend of mine called Rick who had just that week had a baby. He left me a voice note saying, 'Charlotte, I know that when people say it's the most unreal feeling you've ever felt it sounds like a cliché. But it's true. You will never feel this love for anything or anyone – this is going to change your life.' We sat listening to that message over and over again, crying in the pub over our roast dinner. We were about to embark on the biggest journey of our life. And Jake, with tears streaming down his face, looked into my eyes and said, 'I can't thank you enough. I couldn't have done it with anyone else. You are amazing.'

The evening before I was due to go to the hospital, I felt surprisingly calm. I'd never felt this zen before and I was thinking, 'What the hell is going on? Why do I feel this calm?!' We had the film crew for my show with us too and even they were saying, 'Aren't you nervous? What's going through your mind?' But perhaps it was my manifesting psychic sense taking over again, because I just felt this sense of peace all over my body. It might also have been to do with the fact that I knew the pregnancy was going to be over soon and that was filling me with joy! I hadn't exactly had the best pregnancy so I think a part of me was happy that I wouldn't have to get up in the night every half an hour to go to the toilet. That part was finally over. I just felt tranquil. It was so weird.

I slept really well that night (apart from the usual toilet trips) and even when I woke up to wee I didn't once feel nervous or panicked or anxious.

The next day, in the car on the way to the hospital, we were just so excited. It was the strangest feeling. We spent the whole journey taking pictures and videos and when I look back on them now, I can still feel the emotion I was feeling every single minute. I was just swept up with this mood of happiness and anticipation – like no other feeling I had ever known before. Knowing that you are on a journey in a car and that on your way home from that journey you will have a whole new person in your life . . . it's such a mad feeling!

Having the planned C-section made it even more sur-real. Because I guess if you're doing it the natural way, you never quite know when you're going to go into labour – you don't know what's to come. But I knew everything that was happening – it was the most organised plan for the most life-changing thing in the world! It was so weird.

The actual birth

Now, I know it would be a much funnier story if I was to tell you that nothing I had imagined for my perfect birth happened and that *everything was a mad panic*, and all plans went right out of the window. But honestly, IT WAS LIKE NOTHING I COULD EVER IMAGINE IN MY ENTIRE LIFE.

Yes, I nearly fainted twice from having needles put inside me . . .

And also, we fucked up on the playlist situation because Jake left his phone in the room, so we ended up having to put the wrong thing on and Alba emerged into the world to a Ronan Keating song . . .

But all in all my dream scenario – the one that me mam had completely and utterly scoffed at, telling me I was living in cloud cuckoo land to even conceive of it – ACTUALLY CAME TRUE! It was all glorious. Magical. Marvellous. Euphoric. Better than any drug anyone could take. (Not that I've taken any . . .but who needs them when you can have BABIES??!!)

More importantly, despite my worst fears about not being able to bond with my baby – I FELL HARDER IN LOVE THAN I COULD EVER IMAGINE.

We arrived at the Portland and all I remember is being incredibly thirsty because I'd been told I had to go nil by mouth before the operation. We got given our gowns or scrubs to wear and then sat in our room waiting for the doctor to come and see us. I was sitting on the bed looking round the room and thinking how lovely and cosy it was – we had a little settee in the corner that could turn into a double bed for Jake and then there was a tiny little cot beside the bed, just waiting for little baby Alba to lie in it. I looked at Jake and said, 'Does this feel like we're on holiday to you?' and he laughed. We were so excited for what was to come over the next few days and the hospital just felt like this posh hotel where anything and everything was going to happen.

But I was still so calm. The only time that calm wavered a bit was when the anaesthetist, a guy called Mark, came in to explain everything about what was going to happen. He went over the entire procedure in great detail and I found it a bit too much. SHIT. OH FUCK. THIS IS REAL.

I started to get a bit nervous.

It wasn't so much nerves about giving birth, it was just the needle! The thing that threw me was the cannula that he was telling me he'd have to put in my hand. 'Oh, I don't like that bit,' I told him. But he carried on matter of factly, 'So the cannula will have two things attached to it, one for emergency fluids and one in case you lose too much blood.' But I hated the thought of the needle going into the thin skin in my hand – I can't explain why but it did something weird to me. (It wasn't even flashbacks from the ectopic, for most of that I was fainting or losing consciousness because I literally had poisoning in my body from the internal bleeding and was about to die!)

But this cannula was freaking me out. And then there was also the knowledge that I was going to have to have a spinal block – which would be another big needle in my spine to numb the bottom half of my body.

It was time to go down to the operating theatre. Jake was in his scrubs, and I was in my gown, and we had the film crew for my show with us – I think we were causing a right old scene in the hospital! All the nurses were looking at us going past and smiling to themselves. It sounds crazy, but having the cameras there actually made me feel more at ease. I was walking through the corridor and because the cameras were on me and I was talking about what was about to happen I just felt like I was at work. So, it felt really familiar in a strange, bizarre and random way. The two members of the crew who came into the operating room with us were both blokes – Matt and David – and they said they felt lucky and privileged to be with us and to film it all. Matt has got a child himself; I think his wife had a C-section as well. David didn't have any, but he said afterwards he found the whole thing so interesting. It was such a personal thing for everyone to experience together. They said they'd never filmed a birth before – it was a first time for all of us!

There I was, sitting on the operating table and I knew it was time to have the spinal block. And I began to feel all faint. Mark the anaesthetist was incredible. He let me lie down on the bed for a good five minutes and told me to take my time, that we would do everything at my own pace. He held my hand and just said, 'You tell me when you're ready. If you feel faint you can stay there as long as you need because, remember what we spoke about with the spinal block, you need to be really still for me to be able to do that. OK?' Honestly the patience of that team and the care I had in that hospital was amazing, I cannot thank them enough.

Then I sat back up and it was time for the needle in my spine. And when they put it in I honestly did not feel a thing. It was so strange. The sensation that followed was really odd as I could feel my bottom half starting to go numb – but it happened in little patches that I could feel around my body. It happened quite slowly so wasn't something sudden and uncomfortable. My toes were the last thing to go numb and once that had happened, I just had no feeling at all from my neck down.

So there we were in the theatre and it was all about to start. The surgeons were getting their tools ready and suddenly I shouted, 'Hang on! We forgot to put on the playlist!' The playlist. The list of lovely songs I had planned to play – every song chosen for a special reason, all timed to perfection so she would come out to something like Norah Jones 'Come Away with Me'. I looked at Jake expectantly. Jake looked at me with a blank face, 'Shit, I left my phone in the room!' Well, we couldn't exactly stop the proceedings just so Jake could run back to the room could we? So, I said, 'Well we'll have to use my phone then.' The only problem was that the new version of the playlist wasn't on my phone – it was on Jake's. So we only had the depressing version.

This was so typical me.

Plus, all of this mad, panicked discussion was also being filmed by the camera crew! The doctors must have been wondering what the hell was going on!

In the end our beautiful baby Alba entered the world to the one song that I had DELETED from the playlist because I decided it was a bit doom and gloom – Damien Rice's 'The Blower's Daughter'! Or so I thought. When we got back home afterwards I realised that it wasn't even the original version – it was the Ronan Keating version!! Now I don't dislike Ronan but that's not the person I envisaged singing my daughter out of the womb. But I did end up having a little chuckle to myself afterwards though. That could only happen to me!

When the operation started it was another funny sensation. I couldn't feel anything – as in any pain – but I could still feel the doctors tugging about with my insides, them peeling back the layers and rooting around for the baby. It was so odd – a little bit like having a washing machine in place of my stomach, also a bit like a very deep massage! I could feel my body move around and I quite enjoyed it. It felt like when you jump onto a waterbed and then you just bounce around for a little while.

It felt like ages until the baby came out, even though it probably wasn't that long at all. I remember being really impatient and saying to Jake, 'What's going on? Can they hurry up?' I was just so desperate to meet her!

Jake was obviously amazing throughout the whole experience. He sat holding my hand the whole time. It must have been quite scary for him because he was so helpless in that situation and just had to watch it all unfold. I don't think I'd have liked seeing all this big stuff happening to him and not being able to do anything about it. I'd make a rubbish dad!

The whole thing was just so weird. There's a curtain that goes up between you and the surgeons when you have a C-section – but I asked for the curtain to be pulled down for the moment when she was pulled out of me. I watched the whole birth. And I have to tell you, it was the most magical experience of my entire life. If I could go back to that moment and relive the feeling of looking at her emerging from inside me like that I would do it in a second. It was the most euphoric feeling. I have never known anything like it.

I remember waiting to hear her cry for the first time – because that's when you know the baby's alright and everything is safe. Naturally then I cried my eyes out. Jake cried his eyes out. The camera crew even cried their eyes out – so much so that they had to put the two cameras down at one point!

And when I saw her little face for the first time, I just said to Jake, 'She is so beautiful.' She was absolutely perfect. Just like a dream come true. We could never have imagined we would make such a wonderful little special pretty human. She was everything we ever wanted and so much more.

They took her over to the scales to be weighed. Jake was with her and I was getting really impatient as I wanted her with me. I needed to cuddle my little baby for the first time. Come on! Come on! Bring her over to me! Eventually they laid her on my chest, and I couldn't stop kissing and smelling her. It was such a surreal and heavenly moment. I was holding my little girl with my partner by my side and we were cuddling and snuggling together for the first time as a new family. It was just wonderful.

There she was – my little Alba Jean.

When it came to choosing what to call our baby we'd had two options. The first one – which we were dead set on for a couple of months – was Harla. That's because Jake's favourite footballer is Erling Haaland, who plays for Man City. And we thought Harla sounded quite cute. But then I started doing some research and realised it sounded quite similar to harlot – which basically means prostitute. I didn't want people to say Charlotte and Harlot!

I first thought of Alba when I saw Jessica Alba in a movie called *Honey*. I always just loved her second name. I just thought it was pretty on its own. I do think some people's surnames can be dead cute as first names, and it seemed quite unique. So that was it! We chose Jean as her middle name – that comes from my nana. My nana and I were very close as you know. When we named her I never ever imagined Nana wouldn't see her growing up. Thank God she was still there to meet her and see her for the first time. I just wish Alba had been able to get to know that wonderful lady in the same way I did.

Little darling Alba. Just saying her name out loud for the first time and having a face to put it to – what a joy. I think the name Alba is so beautiful. Thankfully she looked like an Alba too. She suits it perfectly. Some people say they choose their baby's name and then the baby pops out and the name feels all wrong. Imagine if you decide you want to call your little boy something like Thor and when he comes out he looks nothing like the powerful superhero you thought he would be, so you decide to call him Martin instead! But luckily our little

Alba looked every inch the popstar, superstar she is going to grow up to be.

Watching Alba sleep on that first night, I wasn't able to keep my eyes off her, I was just gobsmacked at how pretty she was. I couldn't sleep. I didn't sleep a wink all night. All I did was STARE at her and Jake. He was asleep on one bed, and she was in the cot beside me and I stayed up all night taking pictures. My phone nearly burst from the number of videos and photos I took of them both! It was the best time of my life. All I kept thinking was how incredibly lucky I was.

The first twenty-four hours were just a big hazy dream. It was an emotional love rollercoaster, and I was loving the ride! I honestly felt like I was HIGH. Which I couldn't have been because I didn't have any drugs. I didn't have gas and air like you do with a natural birth, I just had painkillers. But I felt so euphoric.

Up until this point I'd been thinking, 'I've got a wonderful boyfriend, I live in a lovely house, I've had some amazing experiences, I've made some amazing friends, I've been on TV and I've travelled the world. What more could I possibly do that would ever top any of the experiences that I've already had? How can life get any better?'

That's genuinely the outlook that I've always had. I've always told myself I need to be so grateful for everything. But now, having had a baby and gone through that experience? This magical amazing whirlwind of a time? It made me realise I hadn't even lived. I hadn't experienced life at all yet. Everything from this point onwards was just going to be a whole new level of amazingness.

MY LIFE HAD JUST COMPLETELY LEVELLED UP!!!

14

My baby is . . .

here and she's coming home

We stayed in the hospital for four days and four nights in total. And if I'm honest, I didn't want to leave! It was the best four days of my life. The care was fantastic, we felt so looked after the entire time. We were surrounded by all these amazing experts who taught us how to look after our child and we felt safe knowing they were there at the touch of a button. They literally gave us classes on how to look after a baby – they showed us everything we needed to remember as new parents. It was like a crash course on looking after a human.

The first visitors we had were Jake's mam Natalie, his brother Reece, and one of Jake's friends. It was really lovely but as I hadn't slept the night before I could hardly keep my eyes open. Jake's mam lives in Spain and got the first flight she could. She's just so wonderful and feels like a second mam and she's offered so much support and help. She said, 'If ever, ever, ever you have a week when you're struggling, I'm here.' Reece is absolutely in love with Alba. He's a proper lad but the minute he laid eyes on her he turned into such a softie.

I couldn't see me mam until we were back in Newcastle as she was too weak from her chemo to travel so we had to wait a whole week which was really tough.

Alba was such a good sleeper at the start. We began to think it was all a bit too good to be true. At one point we looked at her in the cot and said, 'I thought this was meant to be hard?!' Even the midwives who came into the room said, 'We think you've got a sleeping little angel there.' Although they did warn that all babies sleep a lot at first and then after week two everything can suddenly change.

I have so many cherished memories from our time in the hospital – loads of which are based around food! When I was pregnant my appetite had gone weird because I kept feeling sick all the time – but now it was well and truly back with a vengeance.

Eating mac and cheese was a particular highlight, even if it didn't have lobster in it like I'd imagined in my dream birth scenario. I can still taste it now. In fact, the entire Portland menu was mouth-wateringly amazing – we had breakfast, lunch and dinner all included – so we definitely made the most of it. I had pizza one day which was delicious. And oh my God, the chocolate brownie was incredible too.

Feeding Alba for the first time was another moment I will cherish forever. I'd never felt like I wanted to breastfeed, I think because me mam didn't breastfeed me or Nathaniel. And now Alba was here, I knew sharing the feeding would mean Jake would have his own chance to bond with her. The first time Alba took the bottle, she just guzzled the milk like a little woodland creature and looked so happy and content and cute.

That was until two days later we discovered she was intolerant to the milk. I'd been asleep when the midwives came to weigh Alba on a routine check-up. Jake told them just to go ahead and take her, as he wanted to let me have some sleep (seeing as I was fighting it most of the time by just staring at the pair of them). So the midwives took her to the room next door.

Next thing I knew, I was still half dreaming, but I could hear voices, people talking by the side of my bed. 'We've just changed Alba and we've seen that there's a tiny bit of blood in her poo . . .'

I sat BOLT UPRIGHT in bed. I had the sweats and this fear and panic was washing over me.

'What? What's happened? Where is she? Is she OK?'

'We were just doing our routine check-up and found a little bit of blood in her stool. We think she's got a milk intolerance so we need to change her formula.'

My eyes were on stalks. I burst out crying and was inconsolable. Jake was reassuring me, 'Charlotte, it's fine. It's just an intolerance. I had that when I was younger. It's nothing to panic about.' But I was in a right state. I needed to see her and check for myself that she was OK. I wanted her by my side. Honestly, I was on the edge! Jake was doing all he could to calm me down, hugging me and stroking my back. I just felt so helpless and it made me realise just how much I loved this little tiny human. If anything, ever, ever happens to her I will not be able to cope. She is so precious.

Once I'd calmed down, I spoke to the paediatrician who told us that she was intolerant to cow's milk protein. Some babies are lactose intolerant which is the sugar that's in cow's milk, but for Alba it was the cow's milk protein. So she can have cow's milk but it has to be a special kind that's broken down. So they put her on a formula where the cow's milk protein is hydrolysed. Who knew there could be so many different types of milk? And who knew I would learn so much in a few days!?

I know this isn't the same for everyone but even though I was so scared about how I'd react, for me, being a parent has come so naturally. I was so busy worrying, 'How will I know how to do this?' but it came to me like magic. It was as if this maternal instinct suddenly unlocked! And now all I am worrying about is anything bad ever happening to our daughter. I feel a love like I have never felt in my life before.

*   *   *

Then all of a sudden we were sent off out into the world . . . to try and keep this tiny human alive . . . on our own! It was nerve wracking!

We had to drive back to the flat in London, because we had to stay nearby until the final doctor check-up. So we were away from home for another week after the birth. When we'd moved to the flat, we thought we were just going to be there in the lead-up to going to hospital – so we didn't have anything we needed with us. Dad had quickly driven down a week earlier with a Moses basket and the bath (which I now knew how to use thanks to YouTube and the brilliant team at the hospital) – but other than that we had nothing with us in London. After Kate had picked us up from the hospital and taken us back to the apartment, she had to go straight out and buy some steriliser stuff because we didn't have any of that for the bottles either. Everyone has machines these days but ours was at home so we were using these old-fashioned Milton tablets in a bowl for the first few days – like we were living in the Dark Ages!

At last we could take Alba home. The journey was hell though. What should have been a four-and-a-half-hour journey turned into eight and a half hours because we had stupidly timed it to go on a Friday evening – rush-hour weekend traffic. It wasn't the ideal situation with a newborn, but I was desperate to be back home and wanted to leave London as soon as I'd had my stitches checked by the doctor. We had to stop at the services for a feed but we couldn't get out because I didn't want anyone to see us, so we were cramped up in the back of the car. Luckily my bladder has improved tremendously since being pregnant. The second Alba was out of me, the whole thing went straight back to normal! This was a blessing because it meant I didn't have to get out and do a wee by the side of the car for the whole world to see!

When we finally arrived it was like absolute heaven on earth. Walking into our own house where we had a lovely nursery decorated and ready, a proper cot for Alba to sleep in, a proper car seat. All her gorgeous clothes and everything folded in drawers. It just felt amazing.

Seeing me mam and dad for the first time after the birth was SOOOO EMOTIONAL. We all cried our eyes out for ages. Everyone was so in love with her straight away. And so proud and happy. Mam was obsessed with her (she still is!) and couldn't put her down. Dad was a bit nervous at first because he hadn't held a baby for eighteen years – that's how old Nathaniel is now!

Nathaniel came over to see the baby separately a day later. In fact he hates children and babies! We did wonder what he was going to be like when he came round. He walked in and we said, 'This is your niece, Alba,' and he looked at her and said, 'Oh right, that's nice!' and then walked away. Nathaniel has come on so well though, he's grown up so much over the last few years. He's even looking at going to university in York. He wants to do history because that's his favourite subject. Mam and Dad have always wanted him to have independence but now it's come to him leaving the nest I don't think they want him to! I really hope that one day he'll be out in the world making friends, having a girlfriend and living on his own. He needs to start practising some skills though because he still can't even use the oven!

Because I wasn't sure how I'd cope after having a C-section, we'd booked for someone to come and help us out on the first few days. But in the hospital, we had second thoughts because Alba was being such a dream; we thought we were cheating if we got someone to help as she was being so good all on her own. So we spoke to some of the midwives about it and they advised we didn't need one as I was doing so well too. Also we suddenly realised we didn't want a stranger in the house with us, we wanted to be our own little unit. We thought, 'She's perfect, we can do these first few weeks on our own.'

During the first couple of weeks we'd accidentally ended up in a routine so we felt like we were in a good flow when we got home. The first time we ever did her feed was at 3pm so then we started this pattern of every four hours, at 3pm, 7pm and 11pm. It meant we were all asleep by midnight. Alba was waking at 4am but she was a really good girl and was only up for about 30 minutes, so we were back asleep until 8am!

We started off both doing the night feeds together because we love doing everything together – but once we were home me mam said it was a bit silly and we should really take it in turns. I think I'm better at doing the night feed because

I'm good at doing it quietly, whereas Jake is so heavy handed, he wakes everyone up when he's doing it! He hates the technology of everything, so if there's something not working on the steriliser or milk warmer then he's huffing and puffing like it's the end of the world. I laugh and tell him he needs to be a bit more patient!

Instead we booked a maternity nurse to come once a week and be on call if we had any worries medically that didn't feel important enough to ask the doctor. We wanted that peace of mind because of the milk intolerance (and my crazy inconsolable reaction to it!) and also because we found out Alba had a little soft spot on the top of her head which was a bit larger than your average baby because she was lacking a little bit in vitamin D. Our maternity nurse is educated in all this stuff – an expert in milk intolerances and nutrition – and it means we don't need to wait ages for an appointment if we're concerned about anything.

Jake has taken to fatherhood in the most amazing way. I have never seen anyone like him! He has got this maternal instinct that I thought only women had. I was worried I'd not know what to do, but it honestly just seems to have kicked in automatically. But I didn't know it could be the same for dads. It was as if Alba was born and DAD-O-MATIC JAKE LANDED ON PLANET EARTH. Even his mam was in shock. When she came to visit he was having to show her how to hold the baby. 'Where did you learn this?' she was laughing. 'How are you this good?!'

He just shrugged and smiled. 'I don't know. It's my daughter, isn't it? I just need to be there for her always.' Oh, it was so cute.

It was his birthday a couple of days after we got back home and his brother came over. Jake was taking charge of everything, even though he didn't need to. He kept saying, 'I'll do that!' when it came to sorting out Alba with something. I think he just wanted to show off that he knew everything. I didn't mind, I loved him taking control! But it did make me smile. It's like he was saying to everyone, 'Look here – this is how you look after a baby!'

Once we were home we couldn't wait to show Alba off. Having her around just seemed to sprinkle this magical happiness in the air around us – whenever people came around it was like she was shooting out little spurts of joy. Even Jake's mates were messaging him saying things like, 'How is she? What's she doing?' and asking us to send them videos! When Adam and Jamie came to visit her, it was so special. They became OBSESSED with her and kept messaging me wanting updates all the time. They think she's the most beautiful thing ever and I know they're going to spoil her rotten.

Ever since I met them both through working together on In The Style, we knew we were always destined to be friends. When me, Adam and Jamie are together we will not stop laughing. None of us takes life seriously. Adam lets go of all of his inhibitions when he's around me and Jamie is just hilarious. We have had the funniest times ever and just take the piss out of each other. The second I started working with them I knew it was going to last a lifetime. I do feel bad sometimes though – because I get away with a lot more than I would if I wasn't their mate. I think Adam finds it quite hard to shout at me so if I'm late to post promotional stuff, or I've just totally missed something I was supposed to do, he always lets me off.

And I knew they would both have to play a very special role in Alba's life . . .

There was one special visit I was desperate for my little Alba Jean to have and that was to meet her namesake, Nana Jean, for the first time. It was such a special moment I will always cherish. And despite the sadness that was to follow, it will always make me laugh so hard I want to wee myself.

We drove to Nana's a couple of days after we'd got back from London and were settled. I've got a video of them meeting for the first time because I wanted Mam to capture it for our memories – I knew it would be a heartfelt and dead lovely moment. So we pulled up at the house and got out the car and Mam started filming, when we got to the door, I hid round the corner because I was planning to go in and surprise her with Alba once Mam was inside. Nana opened the door and all I could hear was me mam saying, 'What the hell's wrong with your hair?' because Nana had opened the door with her hair all greasy and stringy like she'd covered it with a handful of lard. I couldn't see any of this but I could tell it was funny because of Mam's reaction, and I was trying not to laugh. Mam was saying, 'Have you just washed your hair in conditioner by mistake? What have you done? How long has it been since you washed that? You're not washing it with the right thing!' Mam was laughing but I was still trying to be quiet round the corner. She went inside and got Nana into her usual chair in the living room and then I walked in with Alba to surprise her. I caught sight of her head, which looked like it was covered in wet string, and laughed, 'This was meant to be a really cute video – I can't put this up anywhere with you looking like that!' We were all in stitches. I still had the wound from my C-section so I wasn't meant to be laughing like that, but I couldn't help it. Nana held Alba and I could see how happy she was – she was smiling so much looking at her. But Mam couldn't help coming up with the one-liners so we just kept cracking up. She kept on shouting jokes out about me nana's hair. At one point Alba had her eyes closed and Nana said, 'I don't know why she's got her eyes closed, she's not asleep,' and Mam said, 'It's probably for the best, she doesn't want to see you looking like that.' She just kept with all these witty comebacks after every sentence Nana said. Nana went, 'Oh, look how beautiful her hair is. She's got lovely hair.' Mam said, 'Shame you can't say the same.' I was laughing, but I couldn't laugh because it hurt so much. My whole body was shaking trying not to let a laugh out. I will always remember that moment in such a funny way. Mam washed Nana's hair in the sink before we left that day.

Turned out she was washing her hair in the hair oil you're meant to put on after it's dry!

Even with my nana's hair, and me mam's jokes it was so special to see Nana Jean holding little Alba for the first time. I only wish she could have stayed with us to see her grow up.

Things I've Cried About After Having Alba

You know how I was worried that I'd get this dip in hormones after the baby and then dip into a depression again? Well, I did get a surge of sadness but it was a weird kind of happy sadness. I would cry at things that weren't even sad because I was happy – and then I wouldn't be able to stop. Let me explain:

1. I would look at Alba sleeping and start crying because I didn't want her to change. I'd say to Jake, 'I don't want her to get older! I want to stay in this moment forever.'

2. Then I'd be watching her and Jake sleep and cry because I think I'm the luckiest girl in the world.

3. I'd order sushi and realise I could eat salmon again (which I couldn't eat when I was pregnant), then I'd cry at the realisation that I didn't have Alba in my belly any more. I cried so hard when we ordered sushi. Jake was looking at me saying, 'Are you happy because you can eat salmon again?!' and I said, 'Yes . . . but no . . . I wish Alba was inside me again!'

4. I cried when I looked at my tummy and it started to go down really quickly after the birth because I wouldn't be able to feel her wriggling in there any more!

15

My baby is . . .

the living angel of my Nana Jean ♡

Things with Nana happened so quickly after her first meeting with Alba. It felt as if it was only about a week later that she went into the hospital. This didn't seem a big deal at the time as me nana had been in and out of hospital all her life. She had diphtheria when she was five and so she only had one working lung and it only worked at a really small capacity. When Nana was born, diphtheria was known as a death sentence – it was really incredible that she survived and went on to live such an amazing life. But she always had a bad chest and problems breathing; that's something she struggled with her whole life. To me it was a part of who she was – always in and out of hospital. Whenever a chest infection would come, she would have to go in and be put on a drip with the

223

strongest form of antibiotics going straight to her vein, because tablets just didn't work for her any more. So Nana going into hospital just felt like a really normal thing.

So none of us worried about her this time, we were all just texting her in there to check she was OK. She was replying and saying, 'I'll be out in a couple of days. No need to come and see us. I'll see you when I get home.' But then me mam's friend Sally, who's a really close family friend and looked at me nana like a second mam, popped in to visit and when she walked in, Nana was on the floor. She'd had a fall on the ward and her leg was in a bad way. That's when it started to get bad.

Obviously when you're old, if you fall it can do so much damage because your skin is so thin and fragile your blood vessels aren't protected so well and you bruise and hurt yourself much more easily, and more seriously too. Nana had a hematoma in her leg – it bled so much internally that it was like a huge pool of black blood just lying under the skin. It covered the whole of the bottom half of her leg and her foot was swollen. Last time this had happened to her she was in her sixties, and she'd got an ulcer and was in hospital for a month. But the older you get, the harder it is to fight off, and now she was eighty-five it was always going to be much more difficult.

Her body just wasn't fixing itself like it used to. I went to see her every night. I refused to leave her side. One day when we walked in she didn't recognise us for the first fifteen minutes because she'd gone all delirious, and wasn't letting the nurses take her blood. It was a big shock and I got really worried, because Nana had never been like that before. That's when I realised it was bad. I was sitting with her saying, 'Nana, you are going to get out.' But she looked at me with a worried face and said, 'I'm frightened. I know it's time.' It was awful. As I've told you before, I get death anxiety – I am absolutely terrified. I feel like I can't sleep at night and the emptiness of dying makes me feel like I can't breathe and then suddenly it will be like I'm sinking. From the moment she said that, the anxiety crept back into my brain and started really messing with my head. The fact that she said she was scared really hurt me because I thought, 'What if she's feeling like I do about death?' and she's lying in this hospital, all alone. I couldn't think of anything worse. It really haunted me after.

Obviously, I didn't show her I was feeling all this though, I had to be strong for her. She wasn't letting the doctors and nurses do anything, she wouldn't let anyone take her blood. I kept saying, 'This isn't your time, Nana. You're coming out of hospital soon. You want to spend time with Alba. There's so much more for you to do. I promise you, if you let these people do the tests they need to do they can make you better. You need to let them give you the drip.' We sat with her in the hospital for three hours and she didn't want anyone to touch her. Eventually we persuaded her, but she screamed when the nurse put the needle in. All of her veins were collapsing, she was running out of good veins to take blood from, so it was like torture for her. I heard her wail like I've never heard before, it was more like the sound you get from a child. I was holding her arm and looking towards the wall, because I don't like needles. I just had tears streaming down my face but I didn't want her to see me crying.

After that she got a bit better and wasn't delirious any more. At the next three visits she was up, sitting and talking. One day she was even out of bed and sitting in a chair. I was thinking, 'What the hell? This is amazing!' At one point I even took a little video of her because she ate some corned-beef sandwiches. She was talking as if everything was completely normal.

November 11 was mine and Jake's anniversary, from when he'd first asked me to be his girlfriend in the Maldives. We got a private chef and Mam took Alba for the night. It was my first time drinking properly since being pregnant and when we woke up in the morning my hangover was something else! So I didn't go and see me nana that day, but I was texting her and she was texting back. 'Hi, Nana, have you got your leg elevated like the doctors told you? I'm coming to see you soon.'

Then the next day me mam went to see her and suddenly called me from the hospital. 'Charlotte, you're going to have to come and see Nana now. She is in a really bad way. I think we all need to prepare ourselves.'

I was in shock. 'What? How? I was literally texting her and she was fine.'

'No,' said Mam, 'she's really not in a good way now, she doesn't know who anyone is and is in a world of her own.'

I couldn't wrap my head around it. When I walked into the hospital room Nana just looked straight at me. It was almost an angry look, like a scowl, as if she was thinking, 'Who are you?'

I went towards her, 'Hi, Nana.'

She said, 'Hi, darlin',' as if there was a momentary recognition in her eyes, all of a sudden.

Then she was gone again. And I mean, completely gone. She began talking about random things and was acting as if she was threading an imaginary needle – she was licking the thread and trying to put it through the needle eye. She did that the whole time we were there. She began chatting about Maisie, who was her mam, and she was laughing. I've got to admit, it was nice for me to see her like that. I actually kind of thought, 'Well, if this is how it's going to end, I'd be happy to leave her laughing and smiling about old times.' I'd much rather her be a bit clueless than feeling the fear she had had before.

She started to have these big tremors and shakes in her body, she kept twitching all the time. Mam was convinced she was on her way out, but I kept telling myself she could get over it. I was studying her hands and feet looking for all the signs of dying, like them going blue and purple. None of that was happening. And she was still drinking and eating a bit, which just wasn't like her so I thought that was a good sign. I went home, adamant she was going to pull through. But the next day when I went in, she wasn't better. She had her eyes closed and her lips were starting to get really dry. Because she'd been shaking so much, the doctors told us they were going to give her a drug that would relax all of her muscles, so she wouldn't keep knocking her cannula out. At one point when we went in the room, her hospital gown hadn't been done up properly and her boob was out. So me mam had to quickly tuck it back in. We were laughing at that point because it's the sort of thing me and Mam always did with Nana, like when her hair was all covered in oil. And she'd always laugh too. I said, 'Mam, is it right for us to be laughing at Nana's expense?'

Mam smiled. 'She knows what we're like, Charlotte. She wouldn't care.'

The next day I was on a shoot for Pepper Girls Club and Mam called again, 'It's not good. I spoke with the doctor and she's not going to get better. We have to think about putting her on end-of-life care.'

I couldn't handle it. 'What the fuck?' I was crying my eyes out. I don't know how I finished the shoot. As soon as I could I drove straight to the hospital.

There was a young guy on reception who was a trainee nurse and he said, 'You can't go in just yet, Charlotte. They're just changing her.' I burst into tears. He said, 'Come and sit round here,' and patted the chair next to him. I sat with him and he got a box of tissues out and kept passing them to me, one after another.

'She means so much to me,' I was telling him, 'she's not like a normal nana. She's like a second mam. I literally grew up with her and would sleep at hers three nights a week. She was so cool.'

He said, 'It's my last shift tomorrow but I really do hope for the best for you.'

After that I went into the room and Nana seemed to look at me dead in the eye a couple of times, like there was a flicker of knowing who I was. I sat with her for over half an hour and I told her everything I felt about her and how much I loved her. I told her that I felt so bad that I'd missed spending quality time with her while I was on *Geordie Shore*, because I was travelling everywhere and I was hardly ever home. I was sobbing because I realised I'd missed out on so many years and I felt like I wasn't a good grandaughter because I was just never there. She never watched me on *Geordie Shore*, she'd just say things like, 'I don't think you should do that stuff any more.' But I held her and I told her how much I loved her and how special she was. It was nice to be able to do that and just sit there crying on my own with her.

The following day, Mam and I told the nurse we wanted them to stop the antibiotics and take the cannula out because it was causing her distress and wasn't doing anything any more. We said we'd prefer it so she could have a nice night without ripping it out of her arm all the time and screaming with the injections. We sat next to her and Mam and I were chatting. We were saying we knew we needed to stop the treatment because it wasn't fair, we wanted her to be at peace. I was worried that she could hear us talking and panicked because I didn't want her to think we didn't want her around. Mam said, 'She can't hear – she would move something if she could.' I looked at me nana. Mam was sitting by her bed holding her hand and then Nana started to do this weird thing, her shoulder started to move. I was like, 'What's happening?' Nana started to breathe even more shallowly. Then she stopped breathing for what seemed like ages, probably about thirty seconds and then started again. But we knew this was it, she was taking her final breaths. We held her hands tight and waited. It was so weird, her tongue lolled forward and then she stopped breathing. It wasn't like this huge breath, it just stopped. And I instantly felt this pain in the pit of my stomach. I was so sore with the C-section I was holding on to myself. Mam started wailing, it was a sound so loud and raw. We were calling the nurses, 'She's gone!'

It was just the worst feeling, but at the same time I was so glad I was there and she wasn't on her own. And there was something comforting knowing she was at peace at last. But I was inconsolable. I'd lost me nana. She was the best thing in the world to me. And I was obsessing about every minor detail. Had she heard us talking? Was this her cue to let go? Was she waiting for us to release her? Did she just stop holding on because she knew we'd decided it was OK? I was adamant she knew. I'm not very superstitious or anything but I kept seeing really strange things. There was a clock on the wall in the hospital we used to look at so we would know exactly what time we got there and when she needed to take her medicine. This clock was always absolutely perfectly to time, but the night Nana died it was the wrong time and date. Why was that?! It said it was 4.50pm on 19 December. I knew it might just be me being absolutely ridiculous but it felt significant somehow. I set an alarm for the date and time to see what was happening on that day. Just in case Nana was going to leave me a sign. When it went off nothing was happening so I was a bit disappointed. I don't know what I thought was going to happen – it's not like I was expecting to see Nana Jean flying towards me with angel wings! But then I looked around me and realised I was outside the venue where me mam and dad got married. I don't know if that had any significance but I like to think it was a sign about love. Nana Jean loved Mam and Dad and maybe it was her way of telling me she was OK and that she felt loved and loved us.

When I got back to the house on the day she died, one of the lights above the island in the kitchen started flickering madly. Jake said it could be the bulb but it had never happened before. It was flickering all night and wouldn't stop. And they had never flickered before. For the next two days it was flickering like mad and then it stopped, back to normal. Nothing wrong with it at all. Maybe I was just desperate for anything, a message from Nana to give me some comfort, but it made me feel better thinking she was sending me a sign.

I was a mess after Nana died. I sat in bed from the second I got home after we lost her and I cried like you've never known. But I had to keep reminding myself that Nana was me mam's *mam*. I kept thinking, 'If I'm feeling like this, how the hell is Mam feeling?' I couldn't get out of bed the next morning but Mam picked herself up and went into work, back to packing up boxes in the warehouse for Pepper Girls Club. How was she going to work? Obviously, everyone grieves in a totally different way. I remember hearing someone say that once but I never understood it. Until Nana died, I was quite ignorant of the whole grieving process. I would even go as far as to say that if I had met someone who'd lost someone a while ago and they were suddenly sad, I'd probably have thought, 'Oh, come on. It's been ages!' But now that I've been through it myself, I totally understand it. I just don't know how anyone can ever get over something like that. I don't know whether I ever will. Then I keep thinking, 'Oh my God, I've still got to lose so many people, how the hell am I going to cope?!'

Mam was up, she was out, and she was getting on with life. I kept thinking she's just trying to keep busy so she doesn't think about it so much. She's had the worst year of her life – first to find out she had breast cancer and now she's lost her mam a week before her birthday. It was only a couple of years ago that she lost her dad, Grandad Butch. And that was November too. I remember when that happened she was crying loads and saying, 'I don't want to lose another parent before my birthday!' I wasn't as close to me grandad but I was obviously sad when he died. I cried and cried at the funeral. But I think I was more sad for me mam. I have never felt the level of grief I felt when Nana passed.

Seeing how sad I was, at the end of the week Jake said to me, 'I've got an idea. Why don't we all go and stay at your mam and dad's for the weekend and just be together?' And it was the best thing he could have ever planned. We'd stayed there with Alba before and it had been like a dream being there because the room we stay in is downstairs so we didn't disturb anyone and it's right by the kitchen so I could sneak out and warm up Alba's bottle without having to go all the way downstairs and turn on all the lights, like at our house. So we went over that weekend and we didn't leave until Monday morning. And you know what? We had such a lovely time. It felt really, really special. Even though it was such a sad time we all were together – me, Jake, Alba, Mam, Dad and Nathaniel – and it was so cosy. It was almost like it was Christmas or something. We came together as a family and just had this solid period of time where everyone left us alone – no work, no phone calls, nothing. It sounds weird but it was almost like we were on a three-day holiday. We all knew me nana had died, but we didn't sit and dwell on it. When we spoke about her, we spoke about the funny things, and we ended up sitting and laughing most of the time. Then, if we got sad, we would distract ourselves and sit and watch TV together. One day we got a Chinese and one day we all went on a walk. We knew what had happened, but we didn't speak about it and it was just the most special time. I'll always think of those days dead fondly. It was just what we all needed.

Saying goodbye

The funeral was three weeks after Nana's death. The first week after she died had been horrendous, by the second week I was coming to terms with it and starting to feel better, but then I felt riddled with guilt for feeling better, and then the third week it was as if I was completely back to normal. And I hate saying that because I hate the fact that I acted normal so soon after her death, but I feel like it was my body and mind's way of coping with it. I couldn't beat myself up and be that sad every day any more. I think I almost stopped believing it and convinced myself that if I walked into my nana's house she would say, 'Hi, Charlotte, how are you?' It didn't feel real. It was weird.

And then it was the funeral. I had such anxiety the night before. I was nervous about what I was going to say, about how sad I was going to be, how final it was going to feel. This was the proper goodbye. Mam wanted me to go to see Nana in the coffin before it was closed (some people have an open casket – not sure if it's a religious thing – but we didn't want anything like that). But I told her I'd said my goodbyes already and I didn't want to see Nana like that. Also, I knew my death anxiety would get worse if I saw her. It had just started to calm down and I didn't want to trigger it again. Nathaniel wanted to go and see her as he hadn't had the chance to say goodbye. He is really matter of fact about stuff like that because of his autism; he doesn't get to grips with the emotional side of things, so he is much more measured and scheduled and structured. He had it in his head that he needed to say goodbye to his nana before she left completely and that's just what it was like for him.

Me dad read all the words at the funeral. It was in a crematorium but we didn't have a celebrant speaking because we wanted it to be more personal. Dad had to stand up and tell a story about Nana's life, the sort of person she was, where she grew up and went to school and who her friends were. I don't know how he held it together, but he was so amazing. He put some little jokes in, so even though there were so many tears there was also the odd laugh. My nana loved my dad so much. She literally looked on him as her son, she idolised the ground he walked on, and he felt the same about her as well. He would do absolutely anything for her. And I know for a fact, if she was watching down on him from wherever she is now, she would have been proud as anything and would have loved every single second.

We went to a little pub afterwards to have some drinks and then all of our closest family came to my house. A lot of the family hadn't met Alba yet – including Nana's sister, Letitia. That was so special. Nana had been so excited about being a great-grandma partly because Letitia already had two great-grandchildren and Nana Jean was so jealous! Nana was younger than Letitia and always looked up to her – the name Letitia runs in our family and Nana Jean even named her daughter, me mam, after her! Apparently when they were younger, Nana would follow Letitia around everywhere like her shadow, even when they went to nightclubs and stuff. Nana was dead shy and didn't even kiss anyone until she was twenty-five while Letitia was more outgoing. When Letitia held Alba in her arms, I thought to myself, 'Nana would be proud as punch to see this, she'd be so happy.'

As I watched them together and looked around at everyone gathered in our house, all cooing over baby Alba, I realised that this was a really significant moment. While we had lost someone important in our lives in Nana Jean, we had also gained a new special person in our lives with Alba Jean. It felt like there was an unspoken bond between the two of them, even though they weren't together for long. Nana's memory will always live on in Alba. I will make sure of it.

16

My baby is . . .

growing and changing all the time
(and so am I!)

There have been so many things happen to our family this year that each time a new thing came along and hit me in the face, I almost forget about the last one. I got pregnant and I was so happy, but then me mam got breast cancer and I totally forgot I was pregnant for a bit because I was so focused on Mam and making sure she was OK. Then I had Alba and she spread so much joy around, Mam's breast cancer was forgotten for a bit. But then Nana died and the birth and the breast cancer were just wiped out because there was something new and even more of a big deal to think about. Looking back it's mad how much I was having to deal with at the same time as adjusting to the biggest change of my life – becoming a mam!

Panics and poos!

Anyone looking at my phone bill would think the hospital is one of my best friends. Since I've had Alba, I'm constantly worried that something has happened to her – I get paranoid that she's stopped breathing, or is about to choke, or has contracted some deadly disease in the middle of the night! People say you're always like that with your first born because you just worry as they are so tiny. It doesn't help that whenever you google stuff it always tells you that, whatever the symptoms, your baby is going to die! One evening when she was only a few weeks old, Alba woke up with a rash on her face. Me and Jake thought it was scarlet fever so we rushed her to A&E. It turned out it was just eczema. I think it was because of the cow's milk allergy. Even though her milk is a special kind for intolerances, there's still a tiny amount of cow's milk in there. As she was getting bigger, she was having more bottles, so that's probably why it had come through. And then another day we were panicking because she had been screaming all day long, which isn't like her. Then she did a massive great poo – so big it was all over her neck – and then she was fine!

No one told me that most of your conversations with your

partner as a parent would be about SHIT. *Has she done one? Do you think she needs one? When was the last time she did one?* OH MY GOD, HELP ME, IT'S EXPLODED EVERYWHERE! For someone so small, she can squirt out an incredible amount of poo. And it takes me *and* Jake – two grown adults – to sort it out and clean her up. Once the shit storm has erupted it's no longer a one-person job. The ratio of poo to the size of her body is incredible – it's literally about half her weight. That really is quite impressive when you think about it. Imagine if we shat that much every time we went to the loo – we'd need to have a giant sewer instead of a bathroom.

It's been so cute watching her develop and change as she's grown each week. Even though the changes are small each time, it's amazing watching her learn something new. She started smiling at eight weeks and it felt so incredible finally getting some kind of response to all the mad faces and silly voices me and Jake had been doing at her! She's been holding her head up pretty much since birth – she's so strong! Either that or she's just very nosy – she hates tummy time but when I pick her up and pop her over my shoulder, she calms down instantly. One thing she absolutely hates is the dummy! We've tried it a couple of times when she's been crying loads, just to calm her down, but it just makes her totally mad. She screams and retches. She loves nothing better than sucking her little hand, which is fine by me, because some people say once you've started a baby with a dummy it's hard to get them to stop.

Help me! I'm a new parent!

I have had so much help and support from people following me on Instagram about how to look after Alba – great parenting tips that people have learnt themselves. I know some new mams get really pissed off when they have people telling them what to do – especially if they're in the public eye and fans are giving them unwarranted opinions. But I actually don't mind. Some people can get really offended, because it's like someone else questioning your parenting skills, but at the end of the day, I feel like people are only messaging because they're trying to help. Sometimes what they say can come across wrong, they can seem quite blunt, but it's still coming from a caring place. I love getting the advice and guidance! It's been so good to hear a variety of different people's experiences and cherry pick what I need from it.

A really good example was when Jake, Alba and I were all travelling in the car on our first trip. I posted a video on my socials and some of my followers said I didn't have the handle on properly on the car seat. It was pushed back and it was meant to be up. Neither of us knew it was wrong, but we obviously wanted to get the car seat in correctly, so we were glad someone spotted it before we'd gone more than five minutes up the road. Any advice is welcomed!

One great tip I learnt from Instagram was about how to stop your baby screaming so much when you change them in the night. Those plastic changing mats are really cold and wake them up when they're laid on them, especially in the winter as no one has the heating on full blast in the middle of the night. So the handy tip I got was to always lay the muslin cloth down first, or to use a warmer mat. So now we've got an eco-friendly bamboo mat that is dead soft and cosy and Alba doesn't wake up so much!

The maternity nurse who helped me when Alba was born, told me about these special pillows that you can buy to reduce the risk of your baby getting a flat head because they always sleep on their back. They are mainly used in France but my nurse told me all about them. The pillows let babies lie on their sides completely safely – you can alternate the sides and then put them on their back one night too. Alba loves hers so much – and she hasn't lost one patch of hair!

Well, having said that I have welcomed all the advice I've got, I must give a mention to Milk-bottle-scoop-gate. I posted a photo on Instagram that showed this portable milk powder container for going away or travelling with your baby. In the photo I had put milk powder in the container but I hadn't levelled my scoops, so the measurement was wrong. OH MY GOD, I HAVE NEVER SEEN A REACTION LIKE IT! It was chaos on the comments! I thought I used to get bad comments for my lips but this was next level. I got so much abuse from the 'mam police' it was unreal. The thing was, I wasn't making a bottle, I was putting milk powder in a container to demonstrate how you use it when you're travelling around. I wasn't even putting the powder in an actual bottle. But people were going mad! They were saying things like I was a bad mam and should be more careful. It got really out of control in the end and there were over five hundred comments. It made me feel like shit because no one wants to feel like they are being a bad parent, do they?

Thankfully loads of people started sticking up for me afterwards so in the end there were a load of lovely comments too. People were saying things like:

> Come on guys, leave the poor lass alone! She's a
> new mum – whatever happened to mums supporting
> mums? Kindness and gentle advice costs nothing!

Another one made me smile:

> I'm so glad I was a first time mum 17 years ago
> before social media when you didn't have a dozen
> Supermums telling you how to flipping scoop!

Hangovers and hang-ups

The biggest eye opener for me since having a baby has been how dramatically your relationship changes. Don't get me wrong, it's not for the worse like some people say – we now have a little family unit and nothing can beat that. Jake and

I work together as a team looking after Alba and the love and the bond that we all share as a family is amazing. The difference is that we're no longer boyfriend and girlfriend, pissing about, going on holidays and lazing around! We are now FULLY ON a routine and schedule as soon as the day starts! I was quite shocked at how different it now is between me and Jake because, even though people had warned me about it, I didn't know the change would be so intense. They'd told us that having a baby can come between your relationship a little bit but I'd thought, 'No, that will never happen!' But naturally, it does. You have this whole new realm to your life and your world and priorities completely change – it's quite a shock.

Before Alba, and before I got pregnant, Jake and I were still figuring each other out. We'd go to loads of places, we'd indulge in lovely dinners, we'd spoil each other rotten. Then, all of a sudden, that had to stop because there was a wonderful little person who we now needed to keep happy and alive! It's a constant job – twenty-four hours a day we're doing stuff that revolves around the baby. Even when we do have a second to rest, we've got to sterilise the bottles or do something else before – God forbid – she wakes up and her food isn't there so she's screaming because she's starving! I guess if you breastfeed it might be a bit easier but right now, for us, it's constant! It's hard to think about anything else.

I used to be all over Jake every single second of the day.

I was devoted to Jake and my life revolved around him, showering him with compliments and smothering him with kisses and cuddles – I was like a leech attached to him. But then Alba came along and there was this new energy and another human that I wanted to kiss and shower with my love and affection! He wasn't jealous or anything because the feeling was the same for him. But as soon as she was born she took up so much of our time and attention, we didn't do all those little things any more. I have made a conscious effort to get that compliment card back out for Jake though and make sure he knows how loved and wanted – and lusted after! – he is. Even writing it here is reminding me that it's so important to make that time.

Jake has been much better than me at making sure we have some nights to ourselves. The other day, he said, 'Alba's going to your mam's and we're going away for the night, so pack your bag and make sure you have your swimming costume. I'm taking you to somewhere that you can get dressed up to go for a meal so make sure you pack a nice outfit too.' He's really attentive and I need to take a leaf out of his book because he really makes the effort to keep that spark alive!

Another thing I have noticed from being a parent is that HANGOVERS WITH A BABY ARE SOUL DESTROYING! Well, to be precise, they are the worst thing ever only when you *don't* have your baby with you the next day. After our anniversary, when Mam had Alba, we both woke up with heads like bricks and spent the whole day in bed trying to pull ourselves together. It wasn't just the headache, it was being on the brink of a breakdown because I was riddled with guilt. I felt awful. Physically and mentally. I was saying to myself, 'I'm an awful mam. Why am I doing this? Why have I abandoned my child for booze?' I cried from nine in the morning until four in the afternoon when Mam dropped Alba back at ours. I thought, 'If this is the feeling I am going to get every time, I'm never drinking again.' But the second we got Alba back, we both felt completely fine. I have come to the realisation that having a child is the best hangover cure and that's because you can't just sit around feeling sorry for yourself – you have to get on with it, you have shit to do and it ends up distracting you from your banging head.

Back to being me

My body didn't zip back into shape straight away like you see on Hollywood celebrities who seem to have a baby one day and look like they're about to do a swimwear shoot the next. I was fine with that because I had so many lovely and positive comments after having Alba – everyone was so encouraging and kind to me and told me not to rush back into anything, to enjoy the moment and never worry about how I looked. But I genuinely love exercise, and I've realised that for me it isn't about looking in shape, it is about how it makes me feel in my brain. Exercise definitely gives you a rush and you feel better the more you do.

So I started working out again at the beginning of December and did some every single day without fail. It gave me more energy, even when I felt I had none. I just followed the challenges on my Blitz n Burn app, which helped motivate me as it's got a whole community of other people on there all doing the same thing, so we cheered each other on. To start with I was just doing ten-minute workouts or something simple like a walk (my goals were quite low!).

There were some days when I would be doing Blitz and Burn in the house, then I'd get so hot and sweaty, I'd have to run outside and finish it in the snow – it was snowing everywhere before Christmas remember! Admittedly some of the time, when it got to 10pm and I remembered I hadn't done my exercise for the day I felt sick at the thought of having to drag myself onto the bike. But I always did it, even if it was 11pm by the time I finished! I just kept thinking, 'If I can do this in December, it will be a piece of piss in January!' It's all about self-motivation and setting yourself little goals.

By January, I'd cranked it up and was doing really well. It was a bit annoying exercising to my own videos! I got sick of the sound of my own voice so I made a mental note that next time I film some workouts for the app I will stop talking so much. Luckily we'd added loads of new trainers with their own exercise classes so I didn't have to look at myself the whole time!

Getting back into fitness made me realise just how much it does for me mentally. It's more important for my mind than my body. The powerful effect on my brain is insane. And quite honestly, if I was just doing the exercise to lose weight, I would have stopped after a couple of weeks because I didn't lose a single pound for ages, even though I was working out every single day. If I'd been doing that much exercise before I was pregnant, I'd have lost half a pound a week but post-pregnancy – nothing! As a new mam you have to work so much harder. My belly was so big and swollen for months, it seemed like it would take forever to go.

But I tried to exercise whenever I could because it was bringing me back my sense of self. I didn't realise how sluggish and low I'd got, I thought it was just a side effect from having a baby and lack of sleep. But I hadn't been myself; I couldn't do things that I used to do because I didn't have the same energy levels. I genuinely thought I'd changed as a person in the pregnancy. I was so worried I was never going to get myself back and I thought, 'This is a shame because I loved myself before! I was a great person to be around!' I wanted to be that girl that Jake had met and I didn't want to change just because I'd had a baby. But exercise made me feel like myself again. Half an hour after the first time I worked out I was like, 'Oh my God – I'm back! Yeah!'

Even the camera crew on *Charlotte In Sunderland* noticed

the difference – they came to see me and Jake for some final bits of filming over Christmas and said, 'Wow! You're a changed person!' My message to anyone reading this who can't be arsed to exercise is: you can all find a bit of time in the day to fit in a workout and honestly, you should do it for yourself because you don't realise how much better you'll feel if you do. I'm a better mam because I'm happy, I'm a better girlfriend and I'm an all-round nicer human being.

I was so excited to get back into normal clothes again too. I'd had some amazing maternity outfits – I bought out my own collection with In The Style that completely sold out – but I was so excited to wear stuff again without a big bulging belly. I'd also had to wear some really tight sports bras when I was pregnant too – MY TITS WERE BULGING OUT OF EVERYTHING I WORE! They honestly sprouted from nowhere and were really sore all the time – Jake loved them obviously!

I would describe my style as very casual, sleek and simple. I like leggings and a cap with some sliders, or if I'm going out it will be a nice simple dress. I found a good post-pregnancy look for dressing-up. I wore a long blazer and short dress as it made me feel smart but also hid my belly! When Jake surprised me with a trip away to a spa for Christmas (we do love a nice spa!) I wore a lovely green one when we went out to dinner and matched the giant Christmas tree in the hall.

Out of my whole 'style', the thing I like to change up and mess about with the most is my hair. I like experimenting. I've been brown, blond and once I went all black. But my absolute goal is to have auburn hair. There's a girl I follow on Instagram, she was pregnant at the same time as me and her hair is so shiny and lush and it's a lovely orangey, copper colour. So, watch this space for the transformation!

But the greatest epiphany that came to me after having Alba was to do with my face. One evening, I was sitting watching *Geordie Shore: The Reunion 2022* on TV and I looked at the screen and just thought, 'My face is severely out of proportion – why does it look like that?' I looked like a cartoon character. All I could think was that it must be my lips because my nose is small and my forehead is big, my lips were making my face seem like a really weird shape. I have never thought that before, even though my face has been like that for years. And even though I'd had nearly a decade of comments trolling me because of my 'duck lips' and my 'fish face' I'd never once thought the lips were a problem. I LOVED them! But all of a sudden I felt like there was no need for my lips to be that large and I had the urge to do something about it. I just thought, 'Nah, not having it. This is not my life any more.' I don't know whether it was because I had a daughter – who has amazing lips by the way, it's as if she's been getting injections in the womb – but I just thought, 'I don't want them to look inflated any more. I just want them to look natural.' It's not like I ever got loads of injections before, I had only had to have a little bit put in once a year because my lips just took to the injections really well and held them. But I knew this needed to stop. Jake was devastated. He wanted the lips to stay – obviously he liked them for rude purposes! – but I was adamant. So I booked myself in to get them all dissolved. I'd heard the whole procedure was actually quite painful, but I knew it was the right thing to do.

I was a mixture of nervousness and excitement when I went to the appointment. I had it done by my beloved facial aesthetic lady, Jennifer Smith, who reminded me that she had been doing my lips for over eight years! I have been visiting her for what seems like forever. No wonder they were so big! The procedure did hurt, but it wasn't as bad as I'd feared. Not as painful as having the filler put in there in the first place anyway. When I got home my lips were still really swollen and bruised for about twenty-four hours, but then I looked in the mirror and it was like I had turned the clock back twelve years! Jake was laughing saying, 'All we need is your old nose back and it will be like the first day of *Geordie Shore* again!' I didn't really know what to make of them to start with as it felt so strange. Me mates said I looked like a different person.

I must admit the change has taken a while to get used to. At first, whenever I looked in the mirror, I hated it. I didn't like my lips when I was younger, which was why I had them done in the first place, so why I thought I'd suddenly love the natural look I don't know. I had my first photo shoot a few days after getting them dissolved and I felt so self-conscious and unconfident. I'd been so used to having a big pout and now I felt that I looked like I had a smoker's mouth. When I saw the photos, they weren't as bad as they'd seemed in my head, I just had to learn to pose differently and not smile too much because that's when my lips disappeared! I decided I'd book myself a lip tattoo in blush colour which helps accentuate the shape without messing with it too much. But I know dissolving them has been the right thing to do.

I can't even tell you how many positive messages I had about my new look: 'You look so much better!', 'This is the true beautiful you!' I literally had millions of comments! It was lovely. There was one person who stuck the knife in though and that was another celeb – Ulrika Jonsson in her newspaper column. I didn't see it but Jamie sent it to me and I was shocked that a woman who must have had stuff written about her was now doing it to a fellow female! She didn't give me as much negativity as she gave Katie Price but she was basically saying we'd both messed with our faces. Once again, I thought, 'So much for women supporting women!'

As I look back on the last couple of months of 2022 I can't believe how many monumental changes have happened to me. A baby! New lips! New mindset! New beginnings! Every day I've learnt so much (more than I ever learnt at school!), whether it has been a fellow parent giving me advice on what not to do (!) or learning just how different relationships are after having a baby. It's a good job Jake and I are so strong, because you need to embrace the changes. You have to look after a new little person in your lives and also make sure you look after each other! I've also learnt not to worry about

what my body looks like but to work out for my brain instead.
Oh and I've learnt that there's no point washing your hair very
often because every time you do – your baby will decide to
either puke or poo on it.

A Few Words from Jake on Parenthood

There's so much I feel I've learnt since becoming a daddy to Alba but if I had to boil them down it would be:

Accept that things don't happen instantly.
I've needed to become more patient because I have a child who can't communicate and things don't just 'happen' like they did in what I'm calling 'my previous life' (before Alba came along).

It's opened up a new softer side of me.
I'm more loving than I thought possible. I'm making noises I never would have imagined would come out of my mouth and talking in absolute gobbledeegook.

I'm less stressed.
Things I used to stress about before simply don't matter any more because the little bundle of joy we have in Alba is the most important thing ever. Being a dad has made me the happiest man in the world!

So in a nutshell:

1. Calm down.
2. Worry less.
3. Nappies will get changed .
4. No point stressing about the small stuff.

17

My baby is . . .

a miracle, and I can't wait for more!

Christmas should have been such a cosy and wonderful family time but (a) I always hate Christmas Day anyway – I used to always end up mortal on Christmas Eve and then spend all day with a hangover; (b) Nana wasn't there any more so nothing about it felt right; (c) Jake and I didn't even buy each other anything because we decided to put the money towards a holiday with Alba in Dubai instead and (d) we'd been with Mam, Dad and Nathaniel every other weekend for the last six months so when we sat down to dinner it was just like a normal Sunday roast. I didn't even have a drink over Christmas – that's how crap it was!

One good thing was that Mam had finished her chemo by then. She was meant to have twelve rounds, but she stopped after nine in the end. Chemotherapy is very powerful so it also affects the other organs sometimes. Something it was doing to Mam's liver wasn't good, so they decided to stop – she'd had 90 per cent of it by then anyway and they didn't want to damage her liver. We knew she'd be having radiotherapy in the new year, to properly zap it once and for all, but at least she wasn't having to go to the hospital for treatment over Christmas.

A really great thing that *did* happen over the festive period was that me and Jake asked Adam and Jamie to be Alba's godparents. I'd planned the whole thing for ages and had this special bauble made for the Christmas tree that said, 'Will you be my godparents?' It was meant to be this grand gesture – I was going to take my time getting them to open it – but in the end I had to give it to them in a mad rush. Everything's a mad rush these days with a baby to contend with! They were really, really happy though and we had a dead nice night because they love her so much. She is one lucky girl having them in her life.

One of my best Christmas presents was Holly announcing her pregnancy. She'd actually told me in November but swore me to secrecy because she wasn't announcing it to the world until she was past the three months. She'd begged me to invite her round the house for weeks but I didn't pick up the hint. I kept thinking, 'Why does she want to come over so much? This is a bit out of character!' She never usually wants to move from her own house! I must have been really aggravating because she was desperate to tell somebody and of course that was the reason she wanted to see me.

When I finally invited her, she was absolutely shitting herself, she was shaking. What's weird was that when she arrived she sat down on the same brown sofa that I'd been sitting on when she and Sophie had come over for the MTV filming of me telling them about my pregnancy! So, Holly was in exactly the same scenario. That sofa is now known as the tell-me-you're-having-a-baby sofa! I was not expecting it at all, and was so shocked, but it was the best news ever. It's gorgeous because now we can just sit and talk about baby things all day! Thankfully Sophie is now loved up with Jordan. (When me and Jake met him we made sure he passed the let's-check-he's-not-a-dickhead test as Sophie tends to pick blokes who literally have a cock sticking out of their forehead.) Although Sophie's not ready for kids just yet at least she's not single wanting to mingle and getting pissed off with us two nanas talking about nappies and baby clothes!

Lights, Camera, Action!

I'm really excited for 2023, especially as my new TV show, *Charlotte in Sunderland* comes out in February. As we were filming I was so proud of it. I think of all the times for me to have a camera crew following me, this year has been such a big one. I've only watched a few clips but Kate consumed the whole lot at once and after she'd watched it she called me up and said, 'It's the best thing you've ever done!' I thought it was just her being over-the-top, I mean, Kate is literally my biggest fan, so I took that with a pinch of salt to start with. But then she explained how the crew had captured everything in such depth. They were there for the darkest times (like me mam getting cancer) and also some real highs (like the birth of Alba) – so it's all very raw and emotional. Kate said she thought the bit when we found out about Mam's illness was absolutely heart-breaking. She thinks it's going to do really well, and maybe even win some awards. Of course, me mam will take all the credit if that happens. She will say it's all because of her.

When we first agreed to do the show I remember the producers saying to me, 'We want people to see Charlotte like no one's ever seen her before.' And I was really sceptical because I thought they just didn't realise that I put my life and emotions out on my socials and in my books – surely there's not one part of Charlotte that could be exposed any more! I even felt a bit offended that they didn't know how much TV I'd done in the past. But you know what, they were right. I think it's partly the way it's shot, but also because they were filming me for a whole year and it was literally the most dramatic and life-changing year of my life. Things happened that I thought I'd never have to deal with *ever*. I didn't expect someone I love would get cancer, I didn't know I would be going through that journey or how I would deal with things. I've even surprised myself. Then there was Alba's birth and me nana's death. It's definitely a whole different Charlotte. I didn't once wish the cameras weren't there though. Both me and me mam felt that breast cancer was such an important topic that if the show could help anyone else who's gone through such an absolutely heart-breaking thing, then it was worth it. Whether that's being the person who's had cancer, or their family. Learning how to be around someone who's gone through cancer treat-ment, working out the right things to say – and what you definitely shouldn't say – is such a learning curve. It's so hard for the person who's ill, as they are obviously scared to death, but equally no one really shows what those around them feel or need to do (or not do!).

There was only one scene where I thought afterwards, 'I don't want to watch that back,' and that was when I was having a massive argument with Mam. It was really, *really* bad and afterwards I worried about how I was going to come across. We were in the Pepper Girls Club warehouse, Mam was being so negative and I was trying my best to be positive. Mam said she'd had a really bad week and I thought, 'If I say something a bit more assertively then maybe it will get through.' I thought if I just told her it as it was, that would finally make her think, 'You know what, I need to start turning my thought process around.' So I said to Mam, 'All we keep hearing is that you're going to die and do you know how hard that is for us as a family?' It was coming from a good place but actually it went the complete opposite way. So I am not looking forward to watching that. I don't want to come across as awful but I know the row shows you what families really go through.

As a family we have learnt so much and had to become so resilient. We've literally been on such a rollercoaster with it all. Obviously, it's been hardest for Mam as she's dealing with so much, but the whole family has also had to find a way to cope and to understand how to deal with someone who's got cancer. The worst thing you can say is, 'Don't worry, be positive,' because that's not what the person needs or wants to hear. Mam is still riddled with worry. She still thinks it will come back. I think this is just something she will have to live with now. I've heard a lot of women with breast cancer, or any cancer for that matter, saying how even once it's gone, it's not over. There's always the fear of it coming back, like a never-ending journey. Now we've realised it's something that Mam will worry about every day for the rest of her life and we've just got to be there for her every step of the way.

At least Mam was used to being on camera – I'm always roping her into doing stuff with me. Jake, on the other hand, had never done anything like it before – nor had he wanted to! The first time we did any filming with him he was so nervous and kept asking if what he'd said was OK. But, remember, we had cameras with us for the whole year, so by the end of it he was so natural and relaxed. And everyone on the crew will tell you that we all think he's going to emerge as the hero of the whole show. He is definitely going to be the favourite. Sometimes I would sit there while we were filming and just watch him talk and be taken aback by how amazing he was.

Jake wore his heart on his sleeve the whole way through. He wasn't afraid of crying – he broke down in tears at certain moments when the family was going through bad times – and was just so open and honest. Jake was so raw and natural, it's amazing. He showed that he's not afraid to cry in front of people and he's not afraid to sit down and tell you if he's feeling sad. That's going to be such a breath of fresh air for any man watching. To see a man show that level of vulnerability is something you don't always see on telly. When you think about male suicide rates and how blokes feel they can't talk to anyone . . . I really hope Jake helps at least someone open up and be themselves. This is just another of the million and one reasons Jake's the best dad anyone could ever hope for.

When Jake and I look at Alba we're just so excited about the future and we enjoy every second of being her parents. We're loving it so much that we're planning on another one again soon. Now we've got her in our lives we're not even scared of the responsibilities. I feel such like a mature woman! I think about what she'll be like when she's older, but now I'm excited about it. What's her personality going to be like when she's four or five and she can talk? Is she going to be confident or really shy like I was when I was little (hard to believe I know)? I think she will be dead chatty like Jake and that's going to be dead cute. As you know, I also think she's going to be a pop star as I have already manifested that. I just have this feeling. I knew I was going to have a girl and I just know that she is destined for big things. People don't realise that I actually have quite a good singing voice myself, so I think she's going to take after me and just go for it!

After such a mammoth and life-changing year I cannot wait to see what the future brings for me and Jake. I just know that having him by my side means we can get through any curve-balls life throws at us. Mam is now on the mend and we're planning loads of lovely stuff as a family so hopefully this next few months will be full of happiness and positivity.

Thanks for sticking around through the lows as well as the highs – I hope you'll stay with me for the next few eventful chapters of my life. And who knows, next time we meet I might be married with eight hundred kids!??

Dear Reader

So it's goodbye for now, from me to you,
What a time we've had, with so much that's new,
I've finally met the man who deserves my whole heart
We're completely in love and can't bear to be apart
The good times were huge – we had our precious baby girl!
But grief and hormones have made my feelings whirl
The most life-changing year of my whole life
Now all I need is for Jake to ask me to be his wife! ☺

Charlotte Crosby's Life Goals – aged Thirty-Two (nearly Thirty-Three)

As promised at the start of this book I'm going to do a few more predictions for the future – my next life goals. Let's see how many of these I get right!

1. Have another two kids by the time I'm thirty-five.

I'm not even sure if that's being realistic, as by the time you read this book I could well be thirty-three. Is having three babies in three years physically possible even? I had better get on with it hadn't I? (Jake – let's get jiggy, quick!). I want to have four kids in total. I think I'm going to have girl, girl, girl then boy. Like Victoria Beckham, but the other way round.

2. Buy a plot of land with me mam and dad and build two new houses so we can live side by side.

We've been talking about this already but we just need to find the right location. I think I'll be in Crosby Manor for another three or four years, then we'll start building, and maybe after eighteen months they will both be done and we'll move in. Mam and Dad only live four minutes down the road now, but once we've got our two new houses built they will live four seconds away!

3. Do a voiceover for a character in an animated movie.

Something like *Finding Nemo* but different. I am manifesting being the voice of an emu called Dora.

4. Keep trying to get on *Dancing On Ice*.

Even though they keep ditching me! You never know, I might even get on *Strictly Come Dancing* now I have a show on the BBC. I'll take either!

And finally:
What people think of me . . .
and my response!

I wanted to involve some of you in my book as you always have so many questions and are also so funny and brilliant. So I asked you to send me a few 'assumptions' about me that I could answer for you in here. I had loads of messages and obviously can't print them all but here are some of my faves!

You always wet yourself.

I will admit that from the age of twenty to twenty-eight this was a common occurrence. It happened after every time I'd been out for a drink and was just uncontrollable. Now it's just not even a thing any more! I've honestly had about four years without wetting the bed. I can report that I now have no leaks coming out of any holes whatsoever.

You're very needy.

Yes, this is actually true. I am a very needy girlfriend. Every time Jake goes to the toilet or gets up from the sofa I ask him where he's going. If he wants to go to the shop to get something I say, 'Oh do you have to?' Because I just need to have him there.

You're untidy.

I am SO untidy. There's untidy and then there's me. I am the most awful, messiest person in the world and everywhere I go I leave a trail of destruction. If I have Alba for a day by myself, there will be nappy bags everywhere. I won't have put any in the bin. There will be one bagged at the changing station downstairs, and then more bags upstairs – and Alba's clothes will be scattered all over the house.

You've got no self-confidence at all.

I *do* have self-confidence. I did a live tour where I went out and was just myself. I feel like you've got to be pretty self-confident to do that.

You can't breathe through your nose.

This is true! I think the nose job just messed it all up a little bit.

You don't level your milk scoops.

Ha! Very funny. I didn't level my scoops in that controversial Instagram video but I do actually level them when I make Alba's bottles.

You are a millionaire.

I think on paper, my assets might technically be worth that much, but I don't have a million pounds in the bank. Not even close.

You've been suicidal before.

I've *never* been suicidal. I've been very low before, especially during the early stages of my pregnancy like I mentioned earlier – but I've never wanted to kill myself. Jesus – no!

You don't want to get married.

That is awful. I can't wait to get married! It's my one true goal in life. Actually, I forgot to put that on my goals list! HOW DID THAT HAPPEN?!

You aren't breastfeeding because you don't want to have saggy boobs.

My boobs are done in already. I've had two operations on these fuckers. My boobs were doomed from birth. But my boobs were nothing to do with why I didn't want to breastfeed, I just never felt it was for me

You're quite shy when you meet people for the first time.

Yes, that's true. It depends who it is though. I'm fine with my fans because they've known me for ages, but if I go to a red-carpet event I can't even go over and say hello to the other famous people.

You regret your surgery since having your daughter.

I did dissolve my lips, as you know, but I didn't regret having had them done. They just didn't feel right any more. I *definitely* don't regret my nose job. And if Alba's nose was to grow the same and she wanted to have surgery, I would never stop her from doing that because I know how much I hated mine. But I would never let her have a boob job. Unless she had literally NO boobs at all and they were completely flat. But if she's got a pair of boobies, she's not getting a boob job. There's literally no reason.

You don't pick parcels up.

This must have come from the lady who works in the Post Office near me! That is funny because I don't actually ever collect my parcels. So yes, it's true. And if she wants to drop them off at my house any time, that would be gladly appreciated!

Acknowledgements

Thank you to my family – Mam, Dad and my little brother – for being an amazing support network through the good times and the bad in the biggest year of my life. THANK YOU especially to me mam for being my constant inspiration – a strong, hardworking woman. Regardless of everything that was thrown at you this year, you powered on.

Thank you again to Mr Okaro, and to all of the Portland Hospital team for giving me the best birthing experience I could have ever asked for. I will treasure the memories forever and ever and ever.

Thank you to Nana Jean for being the best nana in the world, for helping to bring me up when I was a little girl, and being the most loving, caring nana ever.

Thank you to Jake, my constant rock! My best friend and my soulmate. Thank you for turning my life upside down and making me the happiest girl in the world! And thank you to your family for being so amazing!

Thank you to my agent, Kate, for always looking after me and guiding me through the last decade – my career on TV and all the other things too! Thanks for being more like my family in so many more ways ! And thank you to everyone at Bold Management!

Thank you to Nav, Ali, the two Davids and all the team at Chatterbox for all your understanding throughout filming what has been such a tough year. And Rachel and Nasfim at the BBC for commissioning *Charlotte in Sunderland*.

Thank you to Lucie Cave, my ghostwriter, for putting up with my pregnancy hormones while going through this whole book lol . And thank you to Sarah and Emma and all the team at Headline for giving me another book!

And thank you to YOU, all my lovely readers, for your continued love and support for which I am so very grateful. x